THE SIKHS

THE SIKHS
Faith, Philosophy & Folk

Text

Gurbachan Singh

Photographs

Sondeep Shankar

Lustre Press
Roli Books

ISBN: 81-7436-037-9

© **Roli & Janssen BV 1998**
Fourth impression 2004
Published in India by Roli Books
in arrangement with Roli & Janssen BV
M-75 Greater Kailash, II (Market)
New Delhi 110 048, India
Tel.: ++91 (11) 29212271, 29212782
Fax: ++91 (11) 29217185
E-mail: roli@vsnl.com; Website: rolibooks.com

Conceived and designed by
Pramod Kapoor
at Roli CAD Centre

Other photographs:
B.P.S. Walia
Ganesh Saili

Printed and bound at Singapore

*To
the evergreen memory
of my parents,*

*Sardar and Sardarni
Mohan Singh*

*of
Rawalpindi*

Previous pages 1: Looking at the Harimandir in awe and devotion . . . Harimandir (Golden Temple), Amritsar.
Pages 2-3: A visitor prostrating himself at first sight of the Harimandir . . . the devotion has to be seen to be believed.
Following pages 6: At a mela . . . A Nihang Singh playfully lifts two youngsters.
Pages 8-9: Harimandir, reverently known as Darbar Sahib to Sikhs and the Golden Temple to others . . . Every Sikh has a desire to pay homage at this shrine at least once in his or her life.

'Akal Sahai' (Immortal Protector). A coin of the Sikh Empire.

'Nanak Shahi' (The Realm of Nanak): a gold coin of the Sikh Empire—Maharaja Ranjit Singh's coinage did not carry his own name.

Contents
— * —

Special Focus on
— * —

ੴ ਸਤਿਗੁਰ ਪ੍ਰਸਾਦਿ ॥
———— ✳ ————

Preface

The Sikh religion is amongst the youngest of faiths, having been founded just about five hundred years ago. Since the gurus all received divine inspiration for their writings, it is one of the revealed religions. While the faith includes some features existing both in Hinduism and Islam, it is not a fusion or synthesis of the two. Essentially, it is a separate faith and has evolved into a separate religion.

Again, though there are similarities with the Bhakti movement, the Sikh faith is not an integral part of the former. There are several differences between the two; Bhakti advocates renunciation, a Sikh's spiritual quest remains within *grahasti* (life of a householder). The focus of worship for Sikhs is the One Supreme, Formless, Eternal Lord and not any icons or human beings. Sikhs do not recognise any caste and believe in universal brotherhood. They are dedicated to *seva* (service) of all, as opposed to the seeking of emancipation or *moksha* of the individual. The Sikhs pray for *sarbat da bhala* (the good of all).

The translations of *Gurbani* wherever occurring in the text are my personal effort. I do not claim any literary merit but, to the extent possible, I have attempted to convey the essential meaning and spirit of the original.

Pictures of the gurus are included in this book. It must be kept in mind, however, that none is a true likeness for no pictures are believed to have been painted during their lifetimes. Each painting reproduced herein projects the artist's conception, the style of the school and the garb of the time.

In this modest endeavour, I have received valuable advice and suggestions from many friends, too numerous to mention individually. I thank them all. My wife and my son, Tejeshwar, a publisher of repute himself, have been my main inspiration and support. My gratitude and blessings for them.

Finally, my sincere thanks to Pramod Kapoor and Bela Butalia of Roli Books for their co-operation, assistance, understanding and, above all, their patience.

GURBACHAN SINGH

The Ten Gurus with Bala (2) and Mardana (7). Tanjore style, late 19th century: Mohan Singh Collection. Nanak (1), Amar Das (3), Arjan (4), Har Rai (5), Teg Bahadur (6), Gobind Singh (8), Har Krishan (9), Har Gobind (10), Ram Das (11), Angad (12).

THE FAITH
———— ✳ ————

Origins

The times were unsettled. Panjab had been on the route of many invasions. The region had seen rulers come and rulers go. At this time it was part of the Sultanate of Delhi where the Lodhi dynasty ruled: first Bahlol Khan, then Sikander Shah followed by Ibrahim Husain, who was defeated at the Battle of Panipat in 1526 by the Moghul invader Babar.

The administration, such as it was, was oppressive. Though largely Muslim, it was discriminatory not only between Muslims and non-Muslims, but also between Muslims of different sects and groupings; the Sunni, the Shia and the Ismaili. There were also the Sufis.

Non-Muslims were required to pay *jizya* (a tax on non-Muslims). Muslims had to pay *zakat*. At times, Hindus were also subjected to a pilgrimage tax. Slavery was in vogue. The rulers at all levels (with some notable exceptions) were unjust and often tyrannical. Life, except for the upper classes, was hard.

Rai Bular was the landlord of the village then known as Rai Bhoi di Talwandi, located 73 kms west of Lahore. It is now known as Nankana Sahib. Mehta Kalyan Chand, popularly known as Mehta Kalu, was the *patwari* (a revenue officer). On 15 April 1469* his wife Tripta gave birth to a son whom they named

*The date is widely accepted though, at some stage, the anniversary of his birth came to be observed on the full moon day of the month of Kartik. One school of thought maintains that the change came about during the reign of Maharaja Ranjit Singh (1799-1839). It was based on the practical consideration that the Sikh peasantry could not, during the wheat harvesting season, manage to celebrate Baisakhi (the spring festival and the birthday of the Khalsa) and Guru Nanak's birth anniversary so close together.

Nanak. They already had a daughter, Nanki, born five years earlier.

Early in his life, **Nanak** showed signs of knowledge and intelligence beyond his years. At the age of six he was placed with Pandit Brijlal to learn Hindi and Sanskrit; later, at the age of thirteen, to learn Persian and Arabic from Maulvi Qutub-ud-Din. To each of his preceptors, he displayed extraordinary sagacity, not only in mastering his instruction but in the questions which he asked. He asserted that without comprehending the essence of knowledge, even a literate person would remain ignorant. His questions confounded his teachers. His homilies impressed others.

From an early age Nanak thought only of the Creator and expressed remarkable insight into the role of the Divine Power on this earth. Incidents recorded about his childhood reveal unusual characteristics which the boy possessed. Amongst the first to recognise his extraordinary qualities were his sister and Rai Bular.

When Nanak was about eleven, his father arranged the customary rite of investing him with the *janeou* (sacred thread worn by upper caste Hindus, particularly Brahmins). When the family *purohit* (priest, also called pandit), Pandit Hardyal, recited the appropriate *mantras* (orisons) and tried to place the thread over the boy's head, he caught the pandit's wrist and questioned him about the purpose of the thread and its efficacy. He effectively refuted the pandit's explanations and declined to wear a symbol which sought to differentiate between man and man on the consideration of caste. He expounded on its ephemeral nature and propounded his own understanding of what is required of human beings. These thoughts were expressed in a *shabad* (hymn) included at page 471 of the *Adi Granth* (literally Primal Book, here the name of the main Sikh scripture):

Woven from the cotton of compassion and the yarn of contentment
With the knot of continence and the strength of truth;
O Pandit, if you have such a janeou *for the soul then put it on.*
This will not break or be soiled; it will neither burn nor perish.

behaviour, not normal in the young, greatly perturbed his father. He thought that the boy may be mentally or physically ill. So, he sent for a *vaid* (physician practising the ayurvedic system of medicine) who, when he came, began his examination by feeling his patient's pulse. He could not detect any ailment. Nanak expressed his reaction which he later embodied in a couplet included in the *Adi Granth* on page 1279:

When the vaid *was called to examine, he began by feeling the pulse.*

The gurdwara *at Nankana Sahib (now in Pakistan), the birthplace of Guru Nanak (1469-1539), the first guru of the Sikhs.*

Mehta Kalu became reconciled to the fact that formal education was not for his son. So he tried to guide him into adopting some calling, in order that he could settle down in life: cattle herding, farming, trading, shop-keeping, accountancy . . . but to no avail. Nanak was totally imbued with his spiritual proclivities. This was manifested in several incidents recorded in the *janam sakhis* (biographies).

Nanak's unusual demeanour (he was aloof, moody, lacked interest in play) and general

The simpleton does not realise that the pain is in the heart.

At this point, Nanak was sent to his sister in Sultanpur. Her husband was in the employ of Daulat Khan Lodhi, the local governor *(nawab)*. He procured a position for Nanak as the *nawab's* storekeeper. Perhaps because he did not want to be a burden on his sister, even though she was older than him, Nanak agreed and began work in order to earn his way.

12

He performed his duties diligently, efficiently and with integrity. Nevertheless, the spiritual quest remained his main preoccupation. He arose before dawn, went to bathe in the nearby stream—the Bein—returned to meditate and pray before his morning meal and on to work. The evenings were spent in spiritual dissertations and singing the praises of the Creator. He began to attract companions for these activities. A childhood friend, Mardana, had also come to Sultanpur. He was to remain a faithful companion and devout follower for the rest of his life. Another childhood playmate, Bala, also joined him and remained with him for long.

Nanak was married in 1487. His wife, Sulakhni, bore him two sons—Sri Chand (1494-1612) and Lakhmi Das (1497-1555)—both born at Sultanpur.

While at Sultanpur, Nanak had a mystic experience. He was then about thirty. One morning, he did not return from his morning bath. There was great consternation in the town. Those who went to look for him found his clothes on the banks of the stream. It was feared that he had drowned. The *nawab* had the stream dredged to recover the body, but in vain. Everyone was distraught. Only Nanki was unperturbed. She was convinced that he would return.

The *janam sakhis* vary on details but are agreed that Nanak had a communion with the Creator. He is believed to have been conducted into the Presence of the Almighty and given a bowl to drink. He was told that it was *amrit* (nectar) which would give him extraordinary powers. He was blessed and given the gift of His Name *(Naam)*, then commanded to return to the world and to propagate the Name of the True One.

Nanak reappeared after three days. He failed to respond to any questions. The following day he declared: 'There is no Hindu, there is no Mussalman.' Whatever anyone asked, the response was the same. After a while he uttered what has come to be known as the *Mool Mantra* (the Fundamental or Primal Orison):

Ik Onkar—There is but One Supreme Protector.
Sat Nam—The only True One.
Karta Purukh—The Creator, All Pervasive.
Nirbhau—Without fear.
Nir Vair—Without rancour.
Akal Murat—Eternal is His Manifestation.

Ajooni Saibhang—Free from birth and rebirth; Self created.
Gur Prasad—Realised only by His Grace.

Then followed an epilogue:

Aad Sach—At the beginning He was.
Jugad Sach—True through the ages.
Haibhi Sach—At present He is.
Nanak, hosi bhi sach—O Nanak, and ever more shall remain so.

The combined dicta became the preamble to the *Japu* (composition of Guru Nanak), the first prayer to be recited by Sikhs every morning. This was the turning point in Nanak's life. Already a realised soul, he was now charged to propagate the Divine Message in a wider milieu. He decided to part from his family, don a mendicant's garb and, accompanied by Bala and Mardana, set forth on his mission. Each journey subsequently undertaken by Nanak is referred to as *udasi* in the *janam sakhis*. There is mention of four main *udasis* over the following twenty years or so. After each round of travel, he returned home for a while before setting off again.

During these travels, he is said to have gone as far afield as Kamrup (Assam), Dhaka and Puri in the east, Rameshwaram and Lanka in the south, Mecca and Baghdad in the west, and Kabul, Kailash and Badrinath in the north, and of course many places on the way. This was in addition to constant travel nearer home. A formidable display of stamina, determination and sense of mission.

Wherever he went, he preached against intolerance, myth and magic. He debunked man-made taboos and barriers of caste. He ridiculed empty ritual and offering of prayer without total devotion and undiluted concentration. He engaged in philosophical debate with the yogis in their *mutths*, the *kazis* and *maulvis* (Muslim priests) in their courts and mosques, the pandits in temples and at places of pilgrimage, the Sufis in their *deras* (dwellings), and with ordinary people everywhere. He taught by precept, logic and example. Many a person did he manage to turn away from evil and wrong-doing and towards purer, simpler and more just living.

On most occasions, the discussion or discourse was followed by his composing and uttering the most sublime and ethereal poetry, almost all of which is included in the *Adi Granth*.

When, accompanied by Mardana, Nanak

arrived at Eminabad he asked for shelter of a carpenter named Lalo. During this time a local official, Malik Bhago, organised a *Brahm Bhoj* (a feeding of Brahmins and holy men). He also invited Nanak who, having come to know of Bhago's reputation as a corrupt man, declined to participate. This incensed Bhago, who had him officially summoned. When he arrived, he was asked why he had spurned the invitation. Nanak sent for a piece of coarse bread from Lalo's dwelling which he held in one hand. In the other, he took savoury foods served at Bhago's feast. It is written that when Nanak closed both fists and squeezed, drops of milk oozed from the hand holding Lalo's bread while blood dripped from the other.

He there recited the following *shabad* in Raag Majh (name of a musical scale), included in the *Adi Granth* at page 141:

Hak paraya Nanka . . .
> Usurped rights, O Nanak
> Are as the flesh of swine for a Muslim,
> And as the flesh of a cow for the Hindu.
> Your Guru or Pir can guide you
> Only if you remain honest.
> Mere talk cannot lead you to heaven,
> Righteous conduct alone can be your salvation.
> Forbidden food, though smothered in
> spices, remains forbidden.
> O Nanak, that which is false, ever remains so.

* * *

When in Hardwar, a major pilgrimage centre on the river Ganga, Nanak saw a group of pilgrims standing knee-deep in the water. Escorted by a pandit chanting *mantras*, they were scooping water from the flowing river and throwing it towards the rising sun. He also waded in, stood alongside the group, and asked what they were doing. The pandit answered that the pilgrims were offering water to their deceased ancestors to assuage their thirst. Thereupon, the guru faced west and, in similar fashion, began to throw water. Asked what he was up to, he replied that he was watering his fields in Kartarpur. They all laughed and ridiculed him. How could the water reach his fields so far away? The guru expressed surprise and wondered how, if the water thrown by him could not reach his fields which were not too far away on this earth, it could reach souls no

longer on this earth and who, in any case, had no physical wants or needs!

* * *

Reaching Puri, the guru and his companions went to the Temple of Lord Jagannath. It was the time of *sandhya* (dusk) and *arati* (worship) was being performed with the customary ritual: *diyas* (oil lamps) on a salver were being waved before the idol, accompanied by burning of incense, blowing of conch shells, striking of brass plates, ringing of bells, chanting, and the waving of whisks. The guru and his companions stood on one side through the ceremony. At its conclusion, an irate pandit came over and upbraided them for not participating in the *arati*. Guru Nanak explained that the Lord of the Universe (Jagannath) is not to be found in wood sculpted by men. He then uttered his conception of *arati* in Raag Dhanasri included in the *Adi Granth* on page 663:

Gagan mein thal Ravi Chand deepak banay . . .
> With the firmament
> as salver, the sun and moon are lamps,
> The stars of the galaxy are pearls
> strewn before Thee;
> Sandal groves of the Malai hills are
> the incense
> While the breezes sway as Thy whisk
> and all the forests of the world
> provide floral offerings.
> What an *arati* it would be,
> O Great Emancipator,
> With endless music and song
> ringing your praises!
> You have thousands of eyes but no eye,
> Thousands of forms yet no form,
> Thousands of feet but no foot,
> Without a nose while having thousands.
> The same light is within everyone;
> the light of God
> Whose Glow illumines all.
> Whatever pleases Thee, O Lord, is the *arati*.
> My soul thirsts for the love of Thy Lotus Feet,
> Bless Nanak, the *saring* (a bird), with
> a drop of Thy Bounty
> So that he may ever abide in Thy Name.

* * *

Facing page: Paath *in peace . . . A corridor in the Harimandir.*

14

On one occasion, the guru and his companions came to a village where they received a cold, even hostile, reception. As they left, Nanak blessed the village. 'May it thrive', he said. At the next village the reception was in complete contrast; warm and hospitable. Upon departure, Nanak said 'May this village become deserted.' Mardana was at a loss to understand this and questioned the Master on the incongruity. Nanak replied that it would be better if the ill-mannered villagers remained together so that they did not contaminate others

were enticed by him to take shelter. During the night, they were invariably robbed of everything, including their lives. Guru Nanak and his companions were also offered shelter for the night. After the evening meal, they commenced *kirtan* (singing of hymns), reciting the praises of the Almighty and of virtuous living. Sajjan waited in vain for his guests to go to sleep. Meanwhile, the words being uttered by Guru Nanak began to have an effect on him until he was overwhelmed by the power and profundity of what he heard. He broke into their room, fell at

Reading the scripture—a granthi *with* chavar *before the* Granth Sahib.

with their example of uncouth behaviour. In the second case, if the villagers scattered, they would spread the example of love, friendship and hospitality, thus benefiting others.

* * *

On the road again, one evening while approaching Multan, Nanak came across a dwelling offering free accommodation and food to wayfarers. It was owned and run by a man named Sajjan. Travellers who appeared affluent

the Master's feet and begged for guidance to salvation.

* * *

Babar, the founder of the Moghul empire, had made forays into northern India before he finally vanquished Ibrahim Lodhi in the Battle of Panipat. Evidently Nanak was witness to the violence and brutality perpetrated by the

Facing page: *Prayer in tranquility . . . tranquility in prayer. A corridor on the upper floor of the Harimandir.*

marauders at Eminabad. He vividly describes the occasion and complains to the Creator. The *shabad* (quoted partially) is at page 360 of the *Adi Granth*:

Khurasan khasmana kiya Hindustan daraya . . .
You patronised Khurasan but tolerated the terrorising of Hindustan.
Not taking the blame Himself, the Creator sent the Moghul against us.
Great havoc was wrought, so much lament; did Thou not have compassion?
O Creator, Thou art the same for all mankind.

And again on page 722:

Jaise mein avay Khasam ki Bani . . .
As I receive the Master's Word, so do I relay it, O Lalo;
He (Babar) has brought sinful hordes in the groom's party from Kabul and forcibly demands the bride.
Decency and morality have gone into hiding and falsehood prevails, O Lalo.
The days of the *kazis* and *brahmins* are past, Satan is now conducting the marriage service, O Lalo.

* * *

On arrival at Mecca, Guru Nanak went to the Ka'aba—the most sacred place of pilgrimage for Muslims. Fatigued after the journey, he lay down at the entrance and fell asleep. The keeper found him in the morning, sleeping with his feet towards the Ka'aba. He was awakened rudely and upbraided for daring to sleep with his feet pointing towards the House of God. Nanak apologised, said that he was a weary traveller, and asked the keeper to do him the favour of taking his feet and turning them in the direction where God did not dwell. To a startled keeper he explained that the entire universe is nothing but God's dwelling.

* * *

Twenty years or so Nanak travelled through unfamiliar terrain, climate and conditions. He met a great number and variety of people. He stayed with humble folk, or slept under the skies, met with the mighty and had discussions with learned men, priests, princes and ordinary people of all religions and persuasions. He visited temples, mosques, pilgrimage centres, festivals and fairs. Wherever he went, he spread his message of love, compassion, truth, righteous living and the Supreme Majesty of the One God. At many places he left a following but the people at every place he visited would long remember the experience.

By 1522 Nanak finally returned home; not to Talwandi but to Kartarpur, the town he had earlier founded on the northern bank of the river Ravi. He was then about fifty-three years old. He settled down there with his family, shed the mendicant's garb and resumed the dress and role of a *grahasti* (householder). Both his parent's died the same year and he attended to their last rites.

Bhai Gurdas (1551-1636), regarded as the first chronicler of the Sikh faith, describes in his *vars* (epic poems) the atmosphere and life in Kartarpur during the final phase of Guru Nanak's life. Resuming a householder's life, the Master continued his teaching. Seated on a cot, he expounded on the Divine Message, spreading understanding and dispelling the webs of ignorance and superstition. Discourses on right living, singing of *kirtan* (prayers), and extolling the Power and Virtues of the Almighty formed part of the daily activities, accompanied by recitations of the *Japuji* (prayer composed by him in praise of the Almighty) in the mornings and *sodar* and *arati* in the evenings.

He set up a community kitchen (the forerunner of the *langar*) subsequently institutionalised by Guru Amar Das, the third guru. Here foodstuffs were donated. Volunteers cooked and served meals to visitors coming to see Guru Nanak. Whosoever came was served without regard to religion or caste.

The Master began to collect a following. People from near and far, hearing of his life and preaching, came to Kartarpur to see him and hear him. They came to be known as Sikhs from the Sanskrit word *shishya*, meaning student or disciple.

In the village of Khadur, near Taran Taran, lived Lehna. Like his father, Bhai Pheru, before him, he was a *pujari* (one who leads the prayer ritual) at the village temple dedicated to Devi, the goddess Durga. Again, as did his father earlier, he conducted an annual pilgrimage of devotees from the village to Vaishno Devi. Setting out on one such journey, he heard about the guru at Kartarpur and took a detour. The

18

day he spent in the congregation made him decide that he need go no further. He parted company with his group and stayed back.

Avidly, he imbibed the atmosphere and teachings at the community in Kartarpur. Before long, he became an ardent devotee. He dedicated himself to the service of the community and of his guru and assiduously absorbed the teachings of the sermons. It is written that Guru Nanak put some of his followers, including both his sons, through some tests. Several incidents are described in the *janam*

The torch had been lit and passed on. It would be for his successors to carry and nurture it.

Evolution

Guru Angad moved to Khadur to continue the mission. Emulating his mentor, he preached the virtues of selfless service, piety and brotherhood. Personally, he led an austere life and a busy one. Several sources, including 'Balwand-Satay *di Var*' on page 966 of the *Adi Granth*, testify to the manner in which he was chosen successor

Implements used for cleansing the sarovar *(pool) laid before the* Granth Sahib *for ritual blessing.*

sakhis. Bhai Lehna unfailingly demonstrated his unflinching obedience, loyalty and devotion. The guru named him Angad to signify that he was an *ang* (limb) of his own body.

Bypassing all others, Guru Nanak named Angad his successor on 15 June 1539. His installation as guru took place on 7 September that year, about two weeks before Guru Nanak's demise. He made Angad more than his successor—he elevated him to be his equal. **Angad** became **Nanak II**.

by Guru Nanak. Sources also record his qualities of generosity, wisdom and humility. He was known for his practice of daily meditation and other austerities.

The routine he followed entailed rising well before dawn and, after a cold bath, meditating until daybreak. Thereafter, *kirtan* was recited in his presence. He then attended to the sick who had come to him for succour and assistance. Later in the mornings, he held well-attended discourses where he preached and expounded

A panel from the Harimandir.

The Sikh Gurus

GURU	Contemporary Rulers in Delhi	Birth	Death	Life Span	Installed Guru (at age)	Duration of Ministry
NANAK	Bahlol Lodhi 1450-89 Sikander Shah 1489-1517 Ibrahim Lodhi 1517-26 Babar 1526-30 Humayun 1530-40	15.4.1469	22.9.1539	70 yrs, 4 months	-	-
ANGAD	Humayun Sher Shah Suri 1540-55	31.3.1504	29.3.1552	47 yrs, 11 months	7.9.1539 (35)	12 yrs, 9 months
AMAR DAS	Sher Shah Suri Humayun 1555-56 Akbar 1556-1605	5.5.1479	1.9.1574	95 yrs, 3 months	1552 (73)	22 yrs, 5 months
RAM DAS	Akbar	24.9.1534	1.9.1581	46 yrs, 11 months	1.9.1574 (40)	7 yrs
ARJAN DEV	Akbar Jahangir 1605-1627	15.4.1563	30.5.1606	43	1.9.1581 (18)	25 yrs
HAR GOBIND	Jahangir Shah Jahan 1627-1658 (1666)	14.6.1595	3.3.1644	51	25.5.1606 (11)	38 yrs
HAR RAI	Shah Jahan Aurangzeb 1658-1707	26.2.1630	30.6.1661	31	8.3.1644 (14)	17 yrs, 5 months
HAR KRISHAN	Aurangzeb	7.7.1656	30.3.1664	8	7.10.1661 (5)	2 yrs, 5 months
TEG BAHADUR	Aurangzeb	1.4.1621	11.11.1675	54	20.3.1665 (44)	10 yrs, 7 months
GOBIND SINGH	Aurangzeb Bahadur Shah 1707-1712	22.12.1666	7.10. 1708	42 yrs, 9 months	11.11.1675 (9)	32 yrs, 10 months

Four panels from the Harimandir. *Guru Nanak (1469-1539) flanked by Mardana (right) and Bala.*

Guru Arjan (1563-1606), compiler of the Adi Granth *and builder of Amritsar.*

Guru Teg Bahadur (1621-75) counselling a group of pandits led by Kirpa Ram of Mattan at Chak Nanki.

Guru Gobind Singh (1666-1708), 'Vah vah Gobind Singh apay Gur chela'.

A panel from the Harimandir showing Guru Amar Das (1479-1574) and the baoli *(well) he got constructed in 1559 at Goindval.*

Genealogical Tables

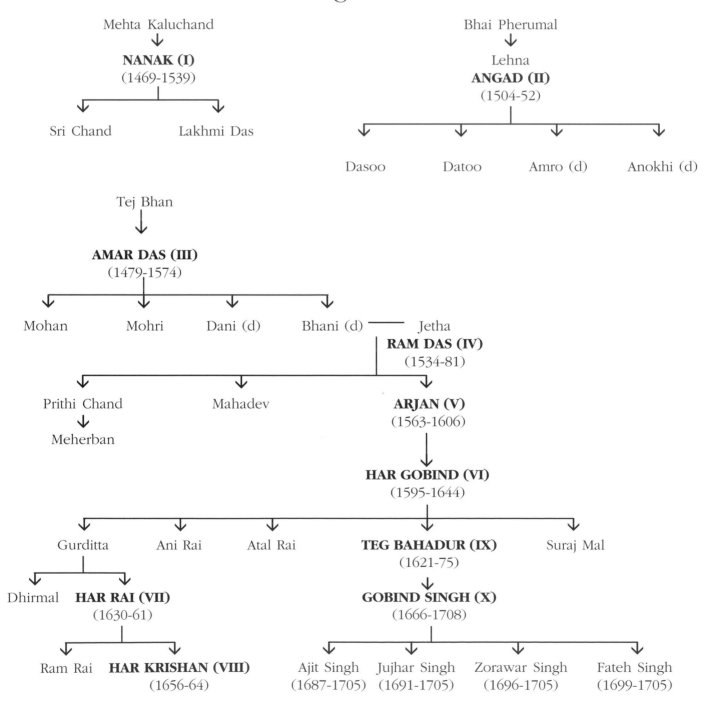

Mehta Kaluchand
↓
NANAK (I)
(1469-1539)

Sri Chand   Lakhmi Das

Bhai Pherumal
↓
Lehna
ANGAD (II)
(1504-52)

Dasoo   Datoo   Amro (d)   Anokhi (d)

Tej Bhan
↓

AMAR DAS (III)
(1479-1574)

Mohan   Mohri   Dani (d)   Bhani (d) —— Jetha
RAM DAS (IV)
(1534-81)

Prithi Chand   Mahadev   **ARJAN (V)**
↓   (1563-1606)
Meherban

HAR GOBIND (VI)
(1595-1644)

Gurditta   Ani Rai   Atal Rai   **TEG BAHADUR (IX)**   Suraj Mal
(1621-75)

Dhirmal   **HAR RAI (VII)**   **GOBIND SINGH (X)**
(1630-61)   (1666-1708)

Ram Rai   **HAR KRISHAN (VIII)**   Ajit Singh   Jujhar Singh   Zorawar Singh   Fateh Singh
(1656-64)   (1687-1705)   (1691-1705)   (1696-1705)   (1699-1705)

on Guru Nanak's *shabads*. The *langar* (kitchen) functioned daily, offering free food to whoever came—without any distinction or barrier. Frequently, he served the food while his wife looked after the cooking. His personal meals were simple; earned by making *munj* (the skin of a reed twisted to make string, widely used in rural Panjab for weaving the base of cots and stools).

Afternoons were invariably for the children, with whom he played and to whom he gave instruction—in reading, writing and the scriptures. Sometimes he witnessed wrestling bouts. In the evenings, again there was *kirtan* and sermons by the guru.

Kartarpur, which had been the centre for Sikhs, gave place to Khadur. Perhaps it was a conscious decision to move away from Kartarpur. The sons of the first guru lived there and might have created problems.

Guru Angad propagated the use of an alphabet, already in use for writing the language spoken by the people. It was derived from *Sharda* and *Takri*, two earlier scripts. He refined it and popularised its use. Some have suggested that Guru Angad invented the script. This, according to Bhai Kahan Singh, is not correct. He cites the *patti* (literally, wooden plaque on which school children learned to write) in Raag Asa composed by Guru Nanak. This is to be found in the *Adi Granth* at page 432, and includes all the letters in that alphabet and contains one which is unique in Panjabi speech. Because this lettering and vowel signs were used to record the sayings and compositions of the gurus, it came to be known as *'gurmukhi'*, that is, 'from the mouth of the Guru'. The language was Panjabi.

Bhai Bala had been Guru Nanak's playmate at Talwandi and later accompanied him on his travels. Guru Angad, being told of Bala, invited him to come to Khadur and narrate events from the first guru's life and travels. Hearing them, he instructed that they be recorded. This account of

Guru Nanak's travels and teachings was inscribed in Gurmukhi characters as they were related in the guru's presence. The book is known as *Bhai Bale Vali Janam Sakhi*. Though it is now controversial—as a consequence, allegedly, of distortions introduced later—it still remains a source of information on the life and times of the first guru.

Guru Angad was an inspired poet who expressed his thoughts mostly in *slokas* (a verse form), of which sixty-three are included in the *Adi Granth*. However, his contribution to the evolution of the faith is more as a consolidator. For nearly thirteen years, he minded the flock, fostered the faith and expanded the circle of adherents.

One of those attracted to Khadur was Amar Das. He became a disciple in 1540 at the age of sixty-one. Over the subsequent twelve years, his devotion and service never faltered. Several instances of his dedication are recorded. Perhaps the most crucial one relates to the occasion when, on a stormy night, Amar Das, as was his routine, was carrying for his guru a container of water taken from the river Beas. He stumbled in the dark but saved the water from spilling. The noise disturbed a woman sleeping in a nearby hut. She rudely remarked that it must be Amru *nithavan* (homeless). When the incident was reported to the guru, he remarked that rather than 'homeless', his follower would be 'home for the homeless'. He added additional epithetic phrases for his disciple: 'honour of the unhonoured', 'strength of the weak', 'protector of the unprotected' and more.

In the course of time Guru Angad, in a manner reminiscent of his own case, chose Amar Das as his successor and asked Bhai Buddha to anoint him as the next guru. Guru Angad passed away on 29 March 1552 and **Amar Das** became **Nanak III** at the age of seventy-three.

Guru Amar Das moved his base to Goindval, a township which he had earlier helped to establish. This was located on the right bank of the river Beas on the main road then running from Lahore to Delhi. In due course it became the first ever place of pilgrimage for Sikhs. He married in 1502 and had two sons, Mohan and Mohri, and two daughters, Dani and Bhani. The third guru was called upon to husband a flock which by then was reasonably well organised

Previous page 23: Guru Ram Das, overseeing enlargement of the pond at Guru ka Chak, of which his son and successor, Arjan, wrote: Ditthe sabhay thhar nahin tudh jiha *(p. 1362,* Adi Granth*). A panel in the Harimandir.*
Facing page: Rotis (unleavened bread) being made for the langar *. . . a daily activity.*

and flourishing. He assumed the task with humility and dedication. He had chosen at a mature age to become a follower of Guru Angad and had imbibed lore about the founder of the faith. His own contribution would be significant.

As torch-bearer and shepherd, he took on his responsibilities with humble fervour. He continued to preach to the daily congregation while undertaking meaningful initiatives of far-reaching consequence. His sermons were in simple language and the similes and examples he gave were related to the daily experiences of

region and wished to see the guru, he was asked to first have a meal in the *langar*.

Guru Amar Das continued steps for reform in social practices. Modified ceremonials for birth, marriage and death were introduced at which *shabads* of the gurus replaced services in Sanskrit. While the people were happy since they could finally understand what was going on, the pandits were understandably angered as the demand for their services declined. The guru condemned and forbade the practice of *sati* (immolation of widows at their husband's pyre)

Nit Nem, *morning prayer in congregation.*

his audience. At the same time, he pursued social and political objectives designed to benefit the people at large and the nascent faith.

The *guru ka langar* became more renowned. In fact it was, to some degree, institutionalised. It was an effective method to foster and emphasize the equality and unity of human beings. Anyone wishing to have an audience of the guru was told: *'pehle pangat, pichhe sangat'*—first sit in a row (and eat), then the meeting. It is said that once, when the emperor Akbar was touring the

amongst his followers, discouraged *purdah* (veiling of women), advocated monogamy, inter-caste matrimony and widow remarriage—radical measures indeed in those times.

Bhani, his youngest child, was born in 1535. She was dear to her father and was devoted to him. She was married to Bhai Jetha, a devotee of the guru who had earlier come to Goindval.

Facing page: A Sikh at prayer: '. . . a Sikh should, whenever possible, recite or hear Gurbani*'.*

26

The fifth guru, Arjan (1563-1606), the first martyr of the Sikhs. Guler; circa 1820: Mohan Singh Collection.

The sixth guru, Har Gobind (1595-1644). Guler; circa 1820: Mohan Singh Collection.

The eighth guru, Har Krishan (1656-64). Guler; circa 1820: Mohan Singh Collection.

The ninth guru, Teg Bahadur (1621-75). Guler; circa 1820: Mohan Singh Collection.

She bore him three sons: Prithi Chand, Mahadev and Arjan.

Lore has it that one morning, when her father was about to sit on a *chowki* (a low stool) to commence his meditation, she noticed that one of its legs was broken. Unflinchingly, she placed the palm of her hand at the point to keep the seat stable for her father and stoically bore the pain. When he got up, he saw blood on the floor and the injury on her hand. Her father was greatly moved, blessed her and offered her a boon. It is said that she asked that future gurus should only be from her family. Though taken aback by this bold request, the guru, having given his word, had to consent. This single incident was to affect the future development of the faith.

In 1559, Guru Amar Das had a *baoli* (well) constructed at Goindval. It has eighty-four steps descending to the water level. Ancient Hindu scholars held that there are eight hundred and forty thousand forms of life through which a soul may have to transit before rebirth as a human, unless it attains *moksha* (liberation). This is part of the Hindu *karmic* belief. Many devout pilgrims to Goindval immerse themselves in the *baoli* eighty-four times, interspersing each dip with reciting the *Japuji* standing on each ascending step. Many Sikhs undertake this as a pious act, others do so in the belief that it will mitigate the severity of the future cycle of rebirth.

As a measure to organise an increasing following, which was also expanding geographically, the guru established twenty-two *manjis*—literally, beds—each of which he put in charge of a *masand* (an appointed representative), each a devout and pious Sikh. These representatives served to look after the local communities, to relay directives from the guru and to collect contributions.

He composed the most sublime and moving poetry, couched in simple language and easily understood metaphor. In 1554, just as he completed a panegyric to the Lord in Raag Ramkali (page 917, *Adi Granth*) consisting of forty verses, he was brought news of the birth of a grandson. He named the baby Anand, the same as the text. This composition is among the

Previous page 29: Guru Gobind Singh out hawking. Lahore with Jammu influence, circa 1900: Mohan Singh Collection.

more familiar *banis* in the *Adi Granth*. It has become *de rigueur* to recite this in an abbreviated version (the first five and the concluding verses) at all Sikh ceremonies. Altogether, 907 of his *shabads* are included in the *Adi Granth*. The twenty-two years he spent tending the faith represent a definitive phase of coalescing and building. Before his demise on 1 September 1574, he nominated his son-in-law, Bhai Jetha, as his successor.

Bhai Jetha was installed as **Guru Ram Das—Nanak IV**. The occasion is vividly described by Guru Amar Das's great grandson, Sunder, who was witness to the scene. The six verses are in Raag Ramkali, known as *Sud* (the call) at page 927 of the *Adi Granth*. Sunder records the guru's last words and actions: how he had become the successor to Nanak's mantle, how he had received the call of the Creator and welcomed it. Addressing those present as his family he explained the call of God; sent for his family members and admonished all not to mourn his passing, instead to recite *kirtan* and have *katha* (discourse); announced his successor—Ram Das Sodhi—and asked his son Mohri and others present to pay obeisance to him. Though extremely brief, this piece is an epic.

Guru Ram Das was forty when called upon to assume his elevated role. Much of his earlier life had, however, been spent in the service of the guru and of the faith he had adopted. He had been active in the *kar seva* (voluntary labour) when the *baoli* was being constructed and had undertaken other assignments for the guru as directed.

In 1574, he was assigned the task of developing a settlement which he named Guru ka Chak, at times referred to as Chak Guru. To the east there was a pond which he had enlarged. The work continued after his succession. The township was later renamed by his son, Arjan, as Ramdaspur and the pool as *amritsar*—the pool of nectar. The city is today known by that name, Amritsar.

In due course, the centre of his activities shifted from Goindval to the new township which, being on the main highway from Delhi to Lahore and further north, became an important trading centre. That a new settlement was founded by the Sikhs and a tank excavated indicates that they now had access to greater resources. Also, that the following was increasing. The contributions for the construction were both in cash and kind. The labour was exclusively voluntary—*kar seva*—whether manual labour, or that of artisans, craftsmen or any other.

Guru Ram Das, like his predecessors, composed *bani*. The *Adi Granth* contains 638 of his *shabads*. Of these, four constitute the *lavan*, which are the central part of the Sikh wedding ceremony (the *Anand Karaj*).

He expanded the arena of activities of the House of Nanak, sent representatives further

rebellious, ambitious and jealous of his youngest brother. The second, Mahadev, had an ascetic nature and had become a virtual recluse. The youngest was closest to his parents and was innately pious and religious. He was consequently the natural choice as successor. Indeed, he seems to have been groomed by his father for the position. However, for the rest of his life he had to face the hostility and machinations of his eldest brother. To contend with these, he had the powerful support of two widely respected elders, Bhai Buddha and Bhai Gurdas. At the

Kar seva *in progress . . . never too young to begin.*

afield to spread the message and kept up the tempo of social reform while consolidating the measures already introduced. The relatively brief period of seven years that he was guru, while not eventful, were nevertheless significant in the evolution of the new faith.

Of his three sons, he chose the youngest, Arjan, as his successor. **Arjan** became **Nanak V** upon the demise of his father on 1 September 1581. Arjan was the youngest of the fourth guru's sons. The eldest, Prithi Chand, was

age of eighteen he had been until then the youngest to become guru. Four successors, including his son, would be even younger.

It is important to note that Arjan was the first guru to have been born in the new faith. Also, that he succeeded to the spiritual centre of his predecessor. The first guru had his base at Kartarpur, the second at Khadur, the third at Goindval and the fourth at Guru ka Chak (renamed Ramdaspur and finally Amritsar). Guru Arjan worked assiduously to consolidate and enlarge the new city which was fast becoming a flourishing commercial town as also a centre of pilgrimage for Sikhs.

The fifth guru achieved much during the twenty-five years that he fostered the faith, its following and its organisation. The first five years were spent in completing projects in and around Amritsar and in touring the neighbouring areas. Wherever he went, he attracted new followers.

The *panth* was now taxed on an organised basis; *dasvand* (literally one-tenth)—originated in the time of Guru Amar Das and implicit even in Guru Nanak's teachings—came to be formalised. All Sikhs were enjoined to contribute, in cash or in kind, one-tenth of their earnings to the guru to be spent on projects or activities for the benefit of the community. The *masands* were to collect the contributions and transmit them to Amritsar. In addition, voluntary labour was liberally and happily forthcoming.

Guru Arjan founded three new towns: Gobindpur (now known as Hargobindpur) on the right bank of the Beas in 1587; Taran Taran, 23 kms south of Amritsar in 1590; and Kartarpur 15 kms north-west of Jalandhar in 1594. This is indicative of both an expanding following and its growing affluence. Santokhsar, a pond north of the present Golden Temple, in Amritsar was bricklined in 1588 and, in the same year—on 12 December—the guru invited Hazrat Mian Mir, a renowned Sufi divine, to lay the foundation of the Harimandir within the complex.

The basic architectural concept of the Harimandir was that of the guru himself. Instead of building it on a high plinth, as was then customary for temples, he had it located on a level lower than the surrounding land. In lieu of the normal single entrance facing east, the new temple had an opening in each of its four walls. The symbolism of these variations dramatically expressed some beliefs of the emerging faith. To reach the House of God a devotee needed to be humble and abase himself. Also, that the temple would be accessible to all—from any side. Some maintain that the four doors betoken equal accessibility to the House of God for the four Hindu *varnas* (castes): *brahmin*, *khshatriya*, *vaisha* and *sudra*.

Until then, Arjan's eldest brother Prithi Chand's animosity, though always present and manifest, had been somewhat subdued. Perhaps he felt that because his brother was childless, the succession would perforce pass to his own son Meherban. The situation changed when, after sixteen years of marriage, a son was born to Arjan's wife, Mata Ganga, in 1595. Prithi Chand was incensed and now became even more hostile. He even connived with the regional Moghul administrators to discredit the guru and impede his mission. But to no avail.

His efforts to woo the community and to turn them against his brother were also unsuccessful. He even made several attempts to have the child poisoned or otherwise harmed. None succeeded. Nevertheless, his self-induced vendetta was relentlessly pursued.

Reports reached the guru that his brother was compiling a selection of verses, including some compositions of his own, and propagating them as the authentic scriptures. Consequently, he now devoted himself to the task of consolidating the *bani* of the gurus into a single volume. He went about his resolve in a methodical manner. Initially, he persuaded his uncle, Baba Mohan, to give him the collection of the writings of the first three gurus that he had with him at Goindval. He also sent emissaries to various places to collect the text of the writings of the first three gurus that individual Sikhs may possess. His father's compositions were already with him. He was himself a gifted and prolific poet. He also collected the writings of many holy men, regardless of origin, and commenced his project.

Seated at the side of Ramsar, a pool a short distance from the Harimandir, he dictated to Bhai Gurdas. The *Moolmantra*, the prologue to Guru Nanak's *Japu*, the guru wrote himself. The rest was written by Bhai Gurdas as indicated by the guru. The volume contains 5,751 *shabads*—4,829 composed by the first five gurus (including 2,312 of his own), 789 by *bhaktas* (devotees) and other holy men. After sustained effort involving rigorous intellectual discipline and gruelling labour, the objective was achieved. As an epilogue the guru composed the *Mundavni* (*Adi Granth*, p. 1429). The initial lines are:

In this salver are three things: truth contentment
and contemplation.
In this also the nectar of the Master's Name Who
is the Support of all.
Whoever partakes of this will be emancipated.

This stupendous anthology completed, the book was ceremonially installed in the Harimandir on 16 August 1604. Bhai Buddha was the first to be entrusted the responsibility of *granthi* (one who attends on the *Granth Sahib,* the Sikh scripture). The Sikhs now had an authoritative scripture of their own.

Guru Arjan was a poet of rare talent and uncommon sensitivity. His compositions have the qualities of mellifluence, sublime beauty and profound spirituality. At the same time, the similes and metaphors, the phrases and imagery,

tamsik, darkness*)* yet is immune to them; it describes contemplation of God's Name *(Prabh Naam)* as the source of bliss; and indicates the requisite conduct whereby humans can aspire for God's Grace and, ultimately, realisation. This *bani* is to be recited as a whole or in instalments, as convenient and as many times as possible.

The new faith had blossomed, with its own scripture and way of life. Its following, though preponderantly to be found in the Panjab, had spread as far as Agra, Kashmir and Kabul. Its distinct identity was spelt out in Guru Arjan's

Ber Baba Buddha. A tree alongside the pool surrounding the Harimandir, under which Baba Buddha sat and supervised kar seva *during construction of the temple and the pool. Baba Buddha was appointed the first* granthi *at the Harimandir, and had the unique privilege of anointing five of the gurus (the second to the sixth).*

are expressed in simple language easily understood by the peasant and the craftsman, the trader and the artisan, the rich and the poor.

The guru's epic composition *Sukhmani* (literally: *sukh,* bliss; *mani,* to the mind) which starts on page 262 of the *Adi Granth* contains twenty-four cantos of eight verses each of five couplets. The *bani* extols the Creator, who has all the qualities (*satvik,* goodness; *rajsik,* energy;

shabad in Raag Bhairav (page 1136, *Adi Granth*):

I do not fast nor observe the month of Ramadan.
I serve Him alone, the ultimate Protector.
The One Master for me is both Gosain and Allah
For I am free of both the Hindu and the Muslim.
I will not go to the Ka'aba for haj
nor to *tiraths* for *puja.*

No *puja* for me, nor *namaz*.
Only the One Formless will I worship.
We are neither Hindus nor Muslims,
We belong to the One, who is
both Allah and Ram.

We should see this as a sequential development of the basic teachings of Guru Nanak and their evolution during the stewardship of his successors up to then.

As the faith evolved and developed so also did opposition to it. Akbar's tolerance and liberal outlook had provided an umbrella for its growth. But this could not prevent covert jealousy and hostility which became overt soon after the emperor's death on 16 October 1605.

Unlike his father, the new emperor, Jahangir, was not an eclectic. In addition, he found cause to have a grievance against the guru. Prince Khusro, Jahangir's son who had rebelled, fled to the Panjab where, according to reports made by the guru's detractors, he received the guru's support and blessings. Those inimical to the Sikhs further encouraged Jahangir's animosity. Within a few months of his accession his ire found expression in action. To quote from his memoirs, *Tuzuk Jahangiri*: 'I fully knew of his heresies, and I ordered that he should be brought into my presence, that his property be confiscated, and that he should be put to death and torture.' The governor of Lahore, Murtaza Khan, was to implement the order. However, according to Sikh chronicles, Chandu Shah—a wealthy merchant and revenue official of the Moghul administration—importuned the governor to be entrusted with the task. Lore has it that Chandu had a personal animus against the guru; namely, a rejected marriage proposal for Chandu's daughter to be betrothed to the guru's young son Har Gobind.

Guru Arjan was subjected to the most horrendous tortures until his body succumbed on 13 May 1606—just seven months after Akbar's death. The Sikhs acquired their first

martyr. A monotheistic, pacifist, non-belligerent philosophy was destined for a metamorphosis.

Har Gobind was installed guru on 25 May 1606, twelve days after his father's martyrdom, when he was not quite eleven years old. Baba Buddha, who had anointed the previous four gurus, placed the *tilak* (auspicious mark) on his forehead. *Masands* had brought a *seli* (a black cord worn over the headdress by some holy men) to be placed around his headgear.

He declined to let it be put on, declaring that the time for *selis* was over. It was now the age to carry weapons. Then he said that his *seli* would be the sword-belt and that, on his turban, he would wear an aigrette—the symbol of royalty. He asked for two swords to wear: one to symbolise *piri* (spiritual authority) and the other *miri* (temporal authority). He was evidently implementing his father's injunctions (as recorded in the *Sri Gur Pratap Suraj Granth*) to ascend to the *gaddi* (throne) fully armed and to have armed men attend on him. Moral and non-violent methods of protest against oppression, intolerance and injustice were set to be replaced by more active and sterner methods of resistance.

As a child, he had been placed under the tutelage of Bhai Gurdas for schooling in the religious texts and *dharma* (moral duty, as also religion), and of Baba Buddha for instruction in the martial arts. He absorbed both assiduously. He sired six children: Gurditta, Ani Rai, Suraj Mal, Atal Rai, Teg Bahadur and a daughter Viro.

Soon after becoming guru, he issued directives to his followers, asking for offerings of horses and weapons. Unlike his predecessors, he began to maintain a retinue of armed Sikhs. The more robust and hardy peasantry began to augment the ranks of the Sikhs, hitherto mainly drawn from the towns.

In 1608-09, at the site facing the main approach to the Harimandir, Har Gobind constructed the Akal Bunga (Abode of the Immortal). Since it became the principal *takht* (throne), it is also known as Akal Takht (Throne of the Immortal). It has become the primary seat of Sikh religious authority and the central point of political assembly. This is the location from where *hukumnamas* (recorded commands) are issued; the *Sarbat Khalsa* (the general assembly of the Khalsa) congregates; and *gurmattas*

Facing page: A sevadar *(attendant) clearing the surface of the pool of flotsam—flower petals, tree leaves, twigs, etc. which have fallen or been blown into the water.*

Following pages 36-37: The Harimandir *(foreground),* the Darshani Deodi *and causeway to the shrine, with the dome of the Akal Takht (far back).*

(resolutions adopted in the presence of the *Granth Sahib*) are adopted.

Reports of the changed style of the sixth guru came as a surprise to the emperor. He had thought that with the torture and execution of Guru Arjan, the Sikhs would have been subdued. Instead, they were becoming stronger and more daring. The guru was dispensing justice amongst his followers, collecting taxes, maintaining armed retainers; like a prince, he went hunting and hawking. His followers addressed him as *sachcha padshah* (true king).

between 1617 and 1619; the exact dates and duration are not certain. The guru had as fellow-prisoners several minor princes and chieftains from various parts of the country. When the time came for his release, he declined to come out unless the other prisoners were simultaneously released. It was agreed that as many as could hold on to his *chola* (a loose ankle length garment) could come out of prison with him. There were fifty-two other prisoners. It is written that the guru had a special *chola* made with fifty-two tassels. All the prisoners were thus able

The Harimandir illuminated at Divali: the festival of lights.

In short, he was acquiring and displaying all the attributes of a political entity; an embryonic state. Emperor Jahangir therefore summoned him to Delhi. On the charge that the fines imposed on his father had not been paid, he was sentenced to imprisonment and incarcerated in the fort at Gwalior.

He remained imprisoned for some months

Facing page: Gurdwaras *are also lit up on Gurpurabs, specially the one falling on Guru Nanak's birthday.*

to gain their freedom with him. That is when he was given the epithet *bandi chhod* (deliverer from bondage).

After his release from Gwalior Fort, Guru Har Gobind travelled to Amritsar. The day coincided with Divali—the festival of lights—observed by illuminating homes. The day acquired a special significance for Sikhs as Amritsar was illuminated to welcome the guru's return. Like Baisakhi, the day became a day of pilgrimage to the seat of the gurus.

Jahangir's attitude towards Guru Har Gobind saw a change; he became more friendly, which enabled the guru to propagate the faith further afield. He travelled in the Panjab, then to Kashmir and later towards the east. In the Garhwal hills he had an encounter with Samarth Ramdas, who later became the Maratha chief Chhatrapati Shivaji's mentor. Seeing the guru fully armed and riding a horse, he asked what kind of a successor he was to Nanak, who had renounced the world. Guru Har Gobind replied that arms meant protection of the poor and resistance against the tyrant. Further, that Baba Nanak had not renounced the world; only *maya* (material wealth) and *homai* (the ego). Samarth is said to have remarked that this answer appealed to him.

Jahangir died in October 1627 and was succeeded by his son Shah Jahan. The detractors and opponents of the guru again became active. They slandered him and carried fabricated tales to the new emperor. Besides, reports reached him of the guru's growing following and of his maintaining armed retainers. These reports added to the consternation at court. Over a period, Shah Jahan's mind was poisoned and he became progressively hostile to the guru.

In the year after his accession, Shah Jahan visited Lahore. Out hunting one day, the emperor's hawk fell into the hands of some Sikhs who took it to the guru. The royal messengers sent to reclaim the hawk were refused its return. The emperor was infuriated and ordered his military commander at Lahore, Mukhlis Khan, to retrieve the bird. The latter marched to Amritsar with a detachment of soldiers. A fight with the Sikhs took place during which Mukhlis Khan was killed. Though this engagement was a minor skirmish, its implications were significant. The Sikhs had, for the first time, militarily challenged the Moghul rulers. Shortly thereafter, Guru Har Gobind left Amritsar, never to return, taking the *Granth Sahib* with him.

There were three further confrontations with the imperial forces—in 1630 with troops of the governor of Jalandhar, Abdullah Khan, at Srigobindpur; the following year at Mehraj with the force of Moghul commander, Kamar Beg; and in 1634 with one of his own renegade soldiers—Painda Khan—who had joined the Moghuls and led an attack on Kartarpur. Soon after these clashes, the guru settled at Kiratpur where he spent the remaining years of his life.

The sixth guru's contributions to the evolution of the faith are significant. First and foremost, the concept of *miri* and *piri* —namely, that the guru, hitherto the spiritual preceptor, would defend the new faith by force of arms when it became necessary.

Then, the introduction of a pennant for his troops, which evolved into the *Nishan Sahib* to be seen at every *gurdwara*; the flag of the Sikhs. It is saffron in colour and displays the Sikh symbol of the *khanda* (double-edged dagger) in black. Even the flagmast is cloaked in saffron cloth. The *nagara*—or kettle drum—used in battle was ultimately to be installed in every *gurdwara*, to be sounded at certain times, for example, when *langar* is ready to be served.

Of Guru Har Gobind's five sons, four had died in his lifetime. The youngest, Teg Bahadur (Mighty of the Sword), had played an important role during the fight at Kartarpur and other conflicts. However, he was retiring by nature and given to meditation and contemplation. The guru later asked his wife to take their son and live in Bakala, a village near Amritsar.

When his time approached, Guru Har Gobind chose his grandson, **Har Rai,** to succeed him. He was the younger son of his eldest, Baba Gurditta, who had predeceased his father. Har Rai acceded to Guru Nanak's spiritual legacy on 8 March 1644. He had been his grandfather's favourite. He was gentle by nature, kind-hearted and devout. He had received guidance and instruction from the Guru himself. He was married in 1640 and had two sons: Ram Rai and Har Krishan.

Guru Har Rai continued to maintain the style of his grandfather, with armed retainers. However, he faced no armed conflict. He took steps to further propagate Guru Nanak's message. He sent several devout and accomplished Sikhs to spread the faith: Bhagat Bhagvan to eastern India, Bhai Pheru to Rajputana and southern Panjab, Bhai Gonda to Kabul, Bhai Nattha to Dhaka and Bhai Jodh to Multan. He himself travelled in the Panjab and Kashmir and attracted more followers. He kept his permanent seat at Kiratpur where he continued the traditions of community prayer, daily discourses, the *langar* and counselling his followers.

Once, when the emperor Shah Jahan fell seriously ill, his son, Aurangzeb, imprisoned him in Agra Fort, and connived with his other two brothers against the eldest, Dara Shikoh, who fled to the Panjab and sought the guru's help.

The latter is said to have deployed a modest force at the ferry at Goindval to delay Aurangzeb's forces who were in pursuit. Dara Shikoh was eventually defeated and killed. Aurangzeb later contrived also to kill his other brothers and ascended to the throne in 1658, while his father was alive. Shah Jahan

Rai went to Dehra Dun where he settled without ever seeing his father again.

Guru Har Rai then nominated his younger son, Har Krishan, to succeed him before he passed away at Kiratpur on 6 October 1661. **Har Krishan** was just over five when he was installed as the eighth guru. Though young in years he displayed an unusual maturity and impressed his followers by his discourses.

His elder brother, Ram Rai, who had been passed over for the succession, sought redress from Aurangzeb for the seeming injustice of his

Nishan Sahib *(flagmast) at Gurdwara Rakab Ganj in New Delhi.*

died in 1666, while still imprisoned.

In addition to the guru's purported action to assist Dara, it was reported to Aurangzeb that the Sikh scriptures contained words derogatory to Islam. Guru Har Rai was summoned to Delhi. He sent instead his elder son Ram Rai. When confronted, Ram Rai distorted a line from the *Granth Sahib* in order, as he thought, to please the emperor. When the incident was reported to the guru, he was incensed and forbade his son ever to appear in his presence. Eventually, Ram

father. The emperor summoned the young guru to Delhi. He arrived in the capital in early March of 1664 and stayed at the house of Raja Jai Singh of Amber. A *gurdwara* known as Bangla Sahib now stands there.

Several instances are recorded to illustrate his intelligence. Cunningham relates one where the child was taken into the royal harem and asked to identify the empress amongst a group of ladies, all equally well dressed. He straightaway identified her and went and sat on her lap.

Another tells of Aurangzeb one day catching hold of both his little hands in one of his and asking what he would do if he were slapped. The guru replied that anyone whose hand the emperor took had nothing to fear; what then had he to be afraid of when the emperor had taken hold of both his hands! Aurangzeb was greatly impressed by his wit and intelligence.

While Har Krishan was in Delhi, an epidemic of small pox broke out in the city. He came out to give aid and succour to those afflicted. In the process, he himself caught the infection. He

conflicts with the Moghul forces. However, he was essentially of an aloof and retiring nature, inclined more towards meditation and contemplation rather than worldly affairs. Nevertheless, he attended to family responsibilities and looked after his mother and his wife. When news reached Bakala of the late guru's dying words, several pretenders set themselves up claiming to be the successor. The most prominent was Dhirmal, the sixth guru's eldest grandson, who had been passed over for succession in favour of his younger brother, Har

Panj Piarey *(with swords) on the steps of Gurdwara Rakab Ganj. Preparatory to leading a Gurpurab procession.*

moved out of Raja Jai Singh's house to a camp on the banks of the river Jamuna. Even while gravely ill he was conscious of his responsibility to name a successor. Before he breathed his last, he uttered the cryptic words 'Baba Bakale'—the Baba, namely, the guru, is at Bakala.

Bakala, a village near Amritsar, is where Guru Har Gobind had sent his wife and youngest son not long before he passed away. Teg Bahadur, in his youth, was an accomplished rider and marksman. He had fought valiantly during the

Rai. There were also others, each with his own *masands*, who were beguiling Sikhs who came in search of the guru.

Makhan Shah, a prosperous Sikh merchant, also came to Bakala. Legend has it that he had vowed an offering of five hundred *mohurs* (gold coins) to the guru for success in a venture. When he arrived at Bakala, he was bewildered

Facing page: *Devotees paying obeisance at Gurdwara Bangla Sahib in New Delhi.*

42

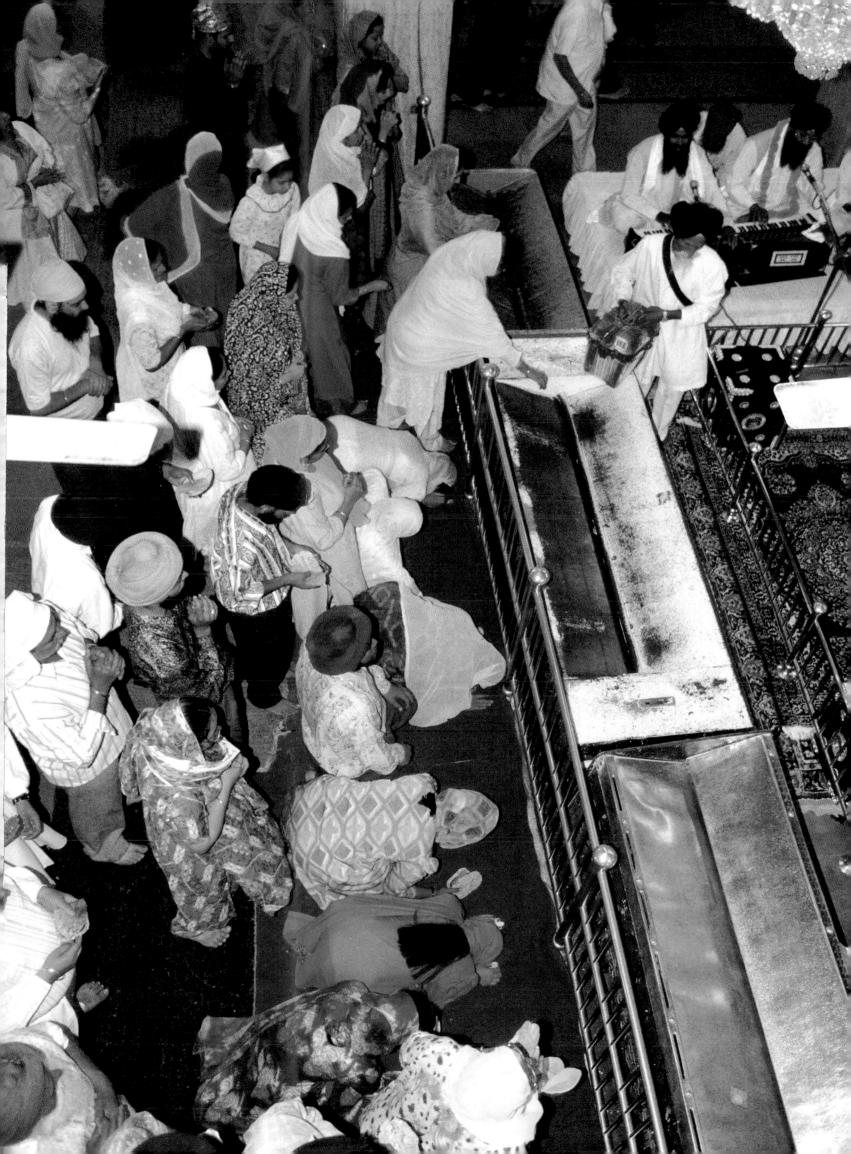

to find several claimants to the *gaddi*. So, he went around the village placing a coin before each 'guru' who nonchalantly accepted the offering.

He was quite perplexed when he was unable to identify the guru. Then he was told of another pious soul in the village who made no claims for himself. Thereupon the merchant sought him out and made his usual offering. He obtained the normal blessing followed by the remark that this was considerably short of the promised five hundred. Makhan Shah was delighted and ran out shouting: *'Guru ladho re, Guru ladho re!'* (I have found the guru).

Hearing this, others flocked to the place, ecstatic at the discovery. Dhirmal's anger drove him to reckless action. He had his men pillage Guru Teg Bahadur's dwelling, and make a murderous attack on his person which, fortunately, was not successful. In retaliation, some Sikhs ransacked Dhirmal's house but the guru had everything restored. At the same time, he deplored their action and lectured them on the virtues of forgiveness.

Guru **Teg Bahadur** assumed the responsibilities of his ministry in earnest, giving spiritual guidance to his followers and administering the affairs of the community. He travelled extensively in the Panjab and neighbouring areas. While at Kahlur (now Bilaspur) he purchased some land from the Raja and founded a new township in 1666 which he named Chak Nanki, after his mother. He shifted there with his family from Kiratpur where he had earlier moved from Bakala. It was renamed Anandpur in 1688 by the tenth guru.

The guru then set off on his travels to the east, taking along his wife and mother. Visiting *sangats* (congregations) along the way, they reached Patna where they stayed a while. Leaving his family there in the care of his brother-in-law, Kirpal Chand, the guru continued his travels eastward visiting Sikh congregations. He went to Dhaka and Chittagong, then north to Assam before heading back to Patna where for the first time he saw his son Gobind Das, now almost three years old. Guru Teg Bahadur travelled more than any of his predecessors since Guru Nanak. It was well that he did so since many *sangats*, several of them existing since the time of the first guru, were looking for

further guidance and direction. He now headed homeward sending his family direct to Chak Nanki while he travelled a circuitous route. He encountered many difficulties both because of schisms within the fold and the hostility of the state. By and large, however, the Sikh *sangats* were supportive.

During this time, while travelling and reflecting, he composed *bani* (compositions, literally, 'that which is made') which are replete with assertions of the transitory nature of life, the futility of attachment to material objects and which extol the ultimate virtue of seeking salvation through meditation on the Name *(Naam)* of the One Supreme Being. One hundred and fifteen *shabads* and *slokas* composed by him are included in the *Adi Granth*.

Aurangzeb's bigotry was scaling new heights. In 1669, he ordered the closure of non-Muslim schools. Places of worship were demolished and mosques constructed on their sites. His regional governors were directed to make forcible conversions. Aurangzeb was reputedly a pious person in his personal life. However, he had imprisoned his father (who languished in confinement for eight years until he died in 1666), and killed all his brothers to attain the throne. Perhaps as expiation he was trying to please the orthodoxy by taking measures to ensure the spread of Islam.

The policy to enforce conversions was apparently initiated in Kashmir. Iftikhar Khan, the governor, commenced implementation zealously. All manner of coercion was utilised. A group of pandits, led by Kirpa Ram of Mattan, came to Chak Nanki to seek the guru's counsel. The guru listened intently to their tale of woe and pondered over the problem. While he sat in deep thought, his young son—just over eight years old—came into the chamber and heard his father say that the problem might be overcome if a truly worthy person were to offer himself as a sacrifice. In childlike simplicity young Gobind wanted to know who could be worthier than his father? The guru was pleased to hear his son speak thus. Thereupon, he asked his visitors to have it conveyed to the emperor that if Teg Bahadur was converted, they would all voluntarily accept Islam. The message was duly conveyed whereupon orders for his arrest were issued.

Anticipating a summons from Delhi, he set out from Chak Nanki, after nominating his son as successor, on 8 July 1675. *En route,* he was taken into custody along with some faithful companions and, under orders of the *faujdar* (military commander) of Sirhind, detained at Bassi Pathanan. There they were confined for over three months and subjected to the harshest treatment. But none succumbed to torture or blandishments. Then they were moved to Delhi where, in sight of the guru, two of his followers—Bhai Mati Das and Bhai Diala—were

(he gave his head but did not display any charism).

Throughout that day, the head and body lay at the place of execution with none daring to claim them. That night there was a storm. In the murky weather, Bhai Jetha retrieved the head and smuggled it to Chak Nanki where it was cremated with due ceremony and solemnity by the young guru. At the site of the cremation a small memorial platform was built at that time. Later a *gurdwara* was constructed there which is also known as Sis Ganj.

Sis Ganj Gurdwara at Delhi. The gurdwara *was constructed at the site where Guru Teg Bahadur was beheaded in 1675 on the orders of the Moghul emperor.*

done to death with extreme cruelty. When this failed to sway him he was asked to perform a miracle to testify to the divine nature of his mission. He refused to even attempt one, maintaining that no one should try to intervene in God's scheme of things. At this the executioner was ordered to perform his duty. On 11 November 1675, the guru's head was severed from his body. At this spot stands Gurdwara Sis Ganj. As later recorded by his son in the *Bachitter Natak, 'Sir diya sirrar na diya'*

Bhai Lakhi Shah and his son picked up the body, put it in an empty cart in which they had brought lime to the city and, under the cover of darkness, took it to their nearby village, Raisina. Since a formal cremation would obviously not have been possible, Bhai Lakhi set his hut on fire, thus burning the body and all his belongings. Gurdwara Rakab Ganj marks the site of this intrepid act.

Here was a holy man, having no quarrel with the state, peacefully propagating a faith. A man of God, who took it upon himself to defend by non-violent means the right of a section of the people to wear the *janeou* and display a *tilak* on the forehead.

His life was taken at the irrational whim of an unjust ruler bent upon coercing a section of his subjects to change their religion. This supreme sacrifice, voluntarily made, when he might well have saved his life by compromising on principles, demonstrates complete faith in and surrender to the Will of God. Also, the superiority of moral force over the physical. This execution, that of a second guru of the Sikhs, was to have significant consequences.

Though there was scarcely any overt demonstration, there was widespread dismay and anger amongst the Hindus who saw the guru's action as a sacrifice for their faith. Many Muslims also expressed disapproval of this execution. Almost the entire Panjab, Sikhs in particular, began to seethe with indignation. The desire for vengeance, already present since Guru Arjan's execution, began to revive. The people at large, especially the sturdy peasants of the region, only wanted a lead and direction. These they were destined to find in the young son of the martyred guru.

Fulfilment

In the early hours before dawn on 22 December 1666, a son was born to Mata Gujri, wife of Guru Teg Bahadur, at Patna. At about the same time, in a village near Karnal, Syed Shah Bhikh—a Muslim divine—looked at the sky and bowed his head towards the east. His disciples questioned him—why, contrary to Muslim custom, had he bowed in the direction of the rising sun? He answered that there had been born in that azimuth a soul who would re-establish morality and destroy evil in this land.

He travelled to Patna to see the newborn. When he saw him, the Syed placed before him two *handis* (clay vessels)—one containing milk and the other water. The infant touched both. The assembled Sikhs asked him the purpose of the offering and the significance of the child's gesture. He replied that his touching both vessels meant that the boy would be impartial towards both Muslims and Hindus.

Named Gobind Das at birth, **Guru Gobind**

Singh grew up to be a sturdy youth with a natural inclination for an outdoor life: riding, hunting, archery, swimming, athletics. At the same time, his intellectual acumen made him a brilliant student who rapidly acquired mastery in Braj, Sanskrit, Persian and his native Panjabi; later, also in Arabic. He assiduously studied the Sikh scriptures, Hindu sacred writings and epics in Sanskrit, and the classics in Persian. Apparently he was deeply impressed by them, particularly those describing contests between the forces of righteousness and evil. He succeeded his father before he was nine years old.

The first ten years or so after his accession were somewhat uneventful. He spent them in study, tending his flock and contemplating on measures to protect and further propagate the new faith. The perceptible increase in his following and their martial deportment caused misgivings amongst some of the hill chieftains ruling areas around Chak Nanki. They were all vassals of the Moghul emperor whose suzerainty they resented but perforce accepted. At the same time there were jealousies and rivalries amongst them.

The Raja of Sirmur invited the young guru to his state. He agreed and stayed at Nahan for a while. Out riding one day, he came across an idyllic spot on the right bank of the river Jamuna. He decided to move from Nahan and set up his own camp there. He named the place Paonta (after the hoofprint—*pav*—made by his horse when suddenly pulled up by the rider) on being struck by the natural beauty of the place.

He stayed at Paonta for nearly four years during which time he gave his followers spiritual guidance and military training. He also spent time in his own literary pursuits and meditation. Much of his writing was evidently done here. He sent some followers to centres of learning in various parts of the country to study other religions and their scriptures. He was desirous that some of them be translated into Gurmukhi, the language of the Sikh scriptures, for the edification of the Sikhs. Poets and savants from afar were attracted to his company, many of whom made valuable contributions to the literature of the time.

The guru himself had a natural skill in prosody. The *Dasam Granth* (separate from the *Adi Granth* and which comprises the tenth guru's verses) contains over 150 variations of metre. The sublimity, beauty, vigour and vitality of his compositions can fully be appreciated only in the original; whether in Panjabi, Sanskrit, Braj, Persian or a *mélange*. Poetry, however, was not his main objective. He used it to express a personal vision of the Almighty. His *bani* eulogises the adoration of the One Supreme Being, enjoining worship of Him alone, while preaching love and the equality of all mankind. He highlights the importance of morality, ethics, sharing and courage in personal conduct, good

Nanak's teachings, he wrote in the *Akal Ustat* (Praise of the Eternal):

> *Dehora maseet soee puja namaz oee*
> *Manas sab ek pai anek ko bharmao hai*
> The mandir and mosque are the same as
> are the *puja* and *namaz*.
> All men are the same but many do not
> understand this.

He emphatically disclaimed divinity by his words in the *Bachitar Natak* (Wonderous Play):

Raagis *performing* kirtan (*singing devotional songs*).

deeds, protection of the weak and resistance to tyranny and injustice. A *swaya* (a poetic form) in 'Chandi Charitra' (a part of the *Dasam Granth*) begins:

Deh Siva bar mohe ehai shub karman te kabhoo na taron . . .

> Grant me this boon, O Lord, that I may never
> shirk from right action.

Echoing and reinforcing the catholicity of Guru

> *Jeh ham ko Parmeshar ucharihai*
> *Tai woh narak kund mein parihai.*
> Whoever refers to me as God
> Will end up in the cauldron of hell.

and continues:

> Regard me only as His servitor and
> Let there be no doubt about this.

In this *bani*, he condemns superstition and idolatry while glorifying *bhagauti* (sword) as a

means of securing justice in the name of God. At the commencement of the *Bachitar Natak* he writes:

I bow with devotion to the Holy sword.

The *Jaap* (verse 52) reads: 'I bow to the Wielder of the sword, the Possessor of all weapons; the ultimate in knowledge and the Mother of all people.' In fact, in the *Akal Ustat*, the Almighty has been referred to as *Sarabloh* (All Steel): He is the destroyer of evil and the punisher of the tyrant. God and the sword, in his conception, would appear to have become conterminous. The sword, however, was not meant for aggression or for perpetrating injustice. It was the symbol of self-respect, to be used only in self-defence or in the cause of righteousness and even then only as a last resort.

It would be pertinent to mention here that the battles fought by the sixth and tenth gurus were in self-defence. Also, that the fight was against tyranny and injustice. Never aggressive in nature. Nor against Muslims or Hindus as such. In fact, the gurus' forces often included Muslim and Hindu soldiers. Further, at no point did the Sikh gurus give expression, in word or deed, of antagonism towards any religion. To the extent that reproof may be discernible, it applies only to empty ritual or prayer without single-minded devotion. This admonition is applicable equally to Sikhs.

The rulers of the hill states were receiving reports of the guru's growing following and of their receiving military training. Also, they took exception to his teachings of equality of all men, disregarding caste. Above all, they became apprehensive of his growing strength and influence. Several rajas combined under the leadership of Fateh Chand of Garhwal and marched against him. A battle ensued at Bhangani, a village near Paonta. The battle, fought in September 1688, ended in defeat for the aggressors. The guru's prestige and influence were further enhanced. He was then not quite twenty-two years old.

Previous pages 48-49: '*Nihangs in their panoply.*' *A procession on the occasion of Hola Mohalla at Anandpur Sahib.*

Shortly thereafter he left Paonta and returned to Chak Nanki which he renamed Anandpur (City of Bliss). He proceeded to build forts there—Keshgarh in the centre and Anandgarh, Lohgarh, Holgarh, Fatehgarh and Taragarh at strategic locations on the periphery. In 1691, there was a battle with a Moghul commander, Alif Khan, at Nadaun which ended in victory for the Sikhs. Several other skirmishes followed resulting mostly in favour of the Sikh forces.

Meanwhile, the guru was receiving complaints with increasing frequency from some Sikh *sangats* of the disreputable activities of the *masands*. In 1698 he issued a *hukumnama* directing Sikhs to no longer acknowledge the *masands* but to communicate directly with the guru and to bring their offerings to Anandpur. He addressed them as his 'Khalsa' (from the Persian word *khalisah*, meaning the land belonging to the sovereign as distinct from fiefdoms).

Concrete form was given to this concept (of a direct link) in a dramatic manner on the first day of Baisakh in 1699. People from far and near had gathered on this day, as had become customary since the time of Guru Amar Das, to pay homage to the guru. Since in the previous year Sikhs had been directed to disregard the *masands*, larger numbers had congregated. Sikhs had been asked to come, as far as possible, carrying arms and on horseback. A massive assembly took place at Keshgarh. While the morning service was in progress, the guru appeared with an unsheathed sword in his hand, a look of intense gravity on his face. He announced to the hushed assemblage that his sword thirsted for blood. Would one of his true Sikhs volunteer to offer his head? There was consternation amongst those who heard the guru's words. Then a stunned silence. The guru spoke again but no one stirred. At his third call, Daya Ram, a *kshatriya*, came forward and offered himself to the guru's will. He was led to a tent pitched nearby. A few minutes later, the guru reappeared before the assembly, his sword dripping with blood. He demanded another volunteer willing to sacrifice his life. Many began to leave. Some went to apprise the guru's mother of his capricious behaviour. However, a second Sikh—Dharam Das, a *jat* (a cultivator caste)—came forward. He, too, was led to the same tent from which, after a brief lapse of time, the guru returned with his sword bloodstained.

He made a third, then a fourth and finally a fifth call for a volunteer willing to sacrifice his life. Mohkam Chand, a calico printer, Himmat, a fisherman, and Sahib Chand, a barber, successively came forward in response to the guru's calls. Each was led into the same tent. The congregation was left nonplussed. Those still remaining waited in trepidation.

A while later, Guru Gobind Singh emerged from the tent leading the five Sikhs who had casteless, martial fraternity. He proceeded next to administer *khande da pahul* or *amrit* (nectar) to them. The five, from different castes, had partaken of *amrit* from the same bowl and been renamed Daya Singh, Dharam Singh, Mohkam Singh, Himmat Singh and Sahib Singh. Caste distinctions had been obliterated and all were given the same suffix 'Singh' (lion) to their names, signifying that they were now brothers. They were required henceforth to wear the five symbols of the Khalsa—*kesh* (unshorn hair), *kirpan* (sword), *kacch* (knee-length drawers),

Leading a school contingent during a procession are five young boys in the garb of Panj Piarey, *with five girls dressed in white.*

volunteered to offer themselves to the guru's sword. They were attired uniformly in saffron coloured robes and turbans of the same colour, each wearing a sword on a belt. The congregation, now much reduced in numbers, stared in disbelief and amazement.

The guru announced that they were the *Panj Piarey* (Five Beloved) who were the culmination of Guru Nanak's revelation. They would form the nucleus of the faith, which he christened Khalsa—'The Pure' or God's Own; a selfless, *kanga* (a small comb) and *kara* (a steel bangle). They were enjoined also to worship and have faith in only one God, to protect and help the weak, resist the oppressor, and to consider all human beings as equal regardless of caste or religion. Other articles of faith were also stipulated. Women were admitted to the initiation and given the name suffix 'Kaur' (Prince).

The initiation ceremony completed, the guru stood before the five and, with folded hands requested them to administer *amrit* to him in the same manner. Having been thus initiated, his name was changed from Gobind Das to **Gobind Singh**. This gesture evoked a poet's exclamation: '*Vah vah Gobind Singh apay Gur chela*' (Hail, Gobind Singh, himself the Guru and the follower).

Learning of this development in the organisation of the Sikhs, the chiefs of the feudatory principalities in the hills were further alarmed. They perceived a threat to both their power and their faith from this militant and

forces of the local chiefs, they laid siege to the fort at Anandpur in May 1705.

The Sikhs resolutely withstood the siege, interspersed with assaults. The inmates of the fort were reduced to dire straits, with scarcities of food and other necessities. Many became so dispirited as to want to leave the fraternity and the fort. The guru was disappointed but agreed on condition that they formally disown him. Forty of them did so, giving him a letter declaring that henceforth neither was he their guru nor were they

Inside the gurdwara *at Keshgarh. The alcove on the right displays some of the arms used by Guru Gobind Singh.*

casteless brotherhood, who had forsworn caste distinctions and who were taught to believe in the basic equality of all humans. They endeavoured jointly and severally to evict the guru from Anandpur, located in the territory of Bilaspur State. Repeated efforts, including armed conflicts, between 1700 and 1704 were unsuccessful. Ultimately, they petitioned Aurangzeb for assistance. Under imperial orders, contingents were sent by the governor of Lahore and the *faujdar* of Sirhind. In concert with the

his Sikhs. They then slunk out of the fort.

The aggressors were vexed at their lack of success against the tenacity of the besieged. In the face of this standoff, the Moghul commander offered, on solemn oath, unharmed passage if the Sikhs agreed to evacuate Anandpur. The offer was accepted and the fort evacuated on the night of 5/6 December 1705. However, soon after the Sikhs came out, the rajas and their Moghul allies attacked them in full force. Many Sikhs were killed and much material was lost, including many precious manuscripts of the guru's writings. Fortunately, the guru escaped together with some Sikhs and managed to reach Chamkaur. The pursuing armies caught up with them and a battle ensued on 7 December 1705.

In the fighting at Chamkaur, the guru's two elder sons—Ajit Singh and Jujhar Singh—and all but the guru himself and five Sikhs, fell in action against great odds. That night the five survivors charged him, under the authority he had himself vested in the *Panj Piarey*, to save himself and to reconsolidate the Khalsa. Being thus compelled the guru, along with three of them, escaped in the darkness. When the fighting resumed on the following day, the remaining two put up a heroic fight before they also fell.

The guru's two younger sons, Zorawar Singh and Fateh Singh, and his mother were betrayed after the evacuation of Anandpur to the *faujdar* of Sirhind. Upon their refusal to convert, the two boys, aged nine and six, were executed on 13 December 1705. Their grandmother died of shock after she came to know of their fate.

Guru Gobind Singh reached Dina, near Faridkot. In a matter of a few days, he had lost his mother, all four sons and countless Sikhs. He was forlorn but not despondent. Here he composed the *Zafarnama* (Epistle of Victory) addressed to Emperor Aurangzeb. Consisting of 111 couplets in Persian verse, it is largely critical of the unjust and unworthy acts of the Moghul regime; condemns the false oaths taken on the *Quran* by the emperor's soldiers; and contains a homily on the duty of kings and the sanctity of solemn pledges. He asserts that, when all other means have failed, resort to the sword becomes justified. The letter emphasizes the supremacy of morality in matters of state as in matters of personal conduct and holds that the means are as important as the ends. Two of his followers were sent with the letter to the south, where Aurangzeb was campaigning.

Meanwhile, the guru enlisted some supporters from the Brar clan and continued his march. He was still being pursued by the Moghul forces. He took a position at Khidrana, by a rainwater pond, where a fierce fight took place on 29 December 1705. The attackers failed to capture their quarry and had to retreat. Crucial support unexpectedly came to the guru from the forty who had disowned him a scant four weeks earlier at Anandpur. When they returned to their homes, they had been chided and ridiculed by their families for their cowardice. In their contrition, they arrived at the site of the engagement under the leadership of a brave woman, Mai Bhago, to redeem themselves. In endeavouring to impede the enemy's advance to the guru's position they sacrificed their lives. After the battle, a critically wounded survivor, Maha Singh, asked the guru for forgiveness for them all and requested that the letter of repudiation given at Anandpur be destroyed. He readily conceded both requests and blessed the martyrs. Their heroic act is recalled in the *ardas* (supplication) as the forty who attained salvation (*mukte*, plural of *mukt*). The place was renamed Muktsar where a resplendent *gurdwara* has been constructed and the pond brick-lined.

Guru Gobind Singh then made his way to Talwandi Sabo, in present day Bathinda district, where he had some respite. Many Sikhs—including poets and savants—joined him there. Much literary activity went on. A recension of the *Adi Granth* was undertaken by the guru himself with Bhai Mani Singh as his amanuensis. Since he stayed (or rested) here for about nine months, the town carries the honorific of Damdama Sahib (literally from *dam*, meaning, to rest). In November 1966, the tercentenary of the guru's birth, the town was declared to be a *takht*—the fifth for the Khalsa.

The messengers sent with the *Zafarnama* had not yet returned. The guru decided to travel south himself. He was in Rajputana when he received news that Aurangzeb had died on 20 February 1707. So, he turned towards Delhi, then to Agra where he met the new emperor, Bahadur Shah. The latter was on the point of leaving for the Deccan as his youngest brother, Kam Baksh, had rebelled and become a contender for the throne. The guru travelled south with Bahadur Shah who, after a conciliatory beginning in talks, found himself helpless to change policies in the face of fanatical satraps as, indeed, of his own preoccupation with fighting for his throne. They parted company at Nanded, a town astride the river Godavari.

Here he came across a *bairagi sadhu* (an ascetic), Madho Das, who was reputed to possess occult powers. He fell under the guru's spell and became his follower. He was initiated into the Khalsa on 3 September 1708 and given the name Banda Singh since he had acknowledged himself as a *banda* (slave) of the guru. He became known as Banda Bahadur and was soon to lead the Khalsa forces in the Panjab wreaking vengeance on those who had wronged the guru and his Sikhs. In the process, he dealt severe blows to the Moghul empire by his numerous successful encounters with the regional forces. 'His great successes gave Sikhism a

and the wound was treated. However, before it healed completely, the guru one day attempted to draw a stiff bow. The strain opened the wound and he bled profusely. He did not recover and passed away on 7 October 1708.

The achievements of Guru Gobind Singh are enormous and should not be underestimated. In a life span of less than forty-two years he brought to culmination a new religion; wrote poetry of indescribable beauty, strength and profundity in four languages; restored self-respect and dignity to an oppressed people; and

Preparing for the initiation ceremony. Five priests doing ardas *at the start of* Amrit Sanskar.

prestige and power which had never yet been associated with it' (see G. C. Narang, p. 111). He was captured in 1716 and cruelly put to death.

Guru Gobind Singh was attracted to the surroundings at Nanded and decided to spend some time there. He was being pursued by two mercenaries commissioned by Wazir Khan, *faujdar* of Sirhind (who was later killed by Banda Bahadur in a battle in 1710). They got to him at Nanded where one evening one of them stabbed the guru. Both assassins were overcome

moulded a fighting force out of a cowed and fragmented society.

There are two major acts of the guru which have had momentous social, religious and, indeed, political consequences. The first is the creation of the Khalsa. By inviting everyone into his fold, by requiring them to drink from the same bowl and by giving them the same appearance and the same suffix 'Singh' to their names, he struck at the caste system to forge a fraternity in which the lowest and highest, men and women, had equal rights—the very essence of democracy.

The second was to ordain that there would be no living successor to him; that the guru would henceforth be the *Granth Sahib*—which contained the message and teachings of Guru Nanak and his successors. He declared that where there were five *(Panj Piarey)* there he would be; that the *sangat* was the embodiment of the guru and that decisions affecting the *panth* were to be taken by *gurmatta*. These were further attributes of democracy.

bard's scroll) by one present, Bhai Narbud Singh, are: 'It is my commandment. Own *Sri Granthji* in my place. He who so acknowledges it will obtain his reward. The Guru will save him. Know this as the truth.' There exist other documents testifying to Guru Gobind Singh's proclamation that the *Granth Sahib* would be the guru in perpetuity.

Thus, despite some aberrations, the Sikhs overwhelmingly accept that the *Adi Granth* is the Guru Eternal. This has been the understanding and conviction of Sikhs since that

Conclusion of ardas *and commencement of* Amrit Sanskar.

Guru Eternal

On 6 October 1708—the day before he passed away—Guru Gobind Singh sent for a coconut which, together with five pice (a currency unit), he placed before the *Adi Granth* and made obeisance to it. He then declared that the line of living gurus had come to an end and that henceforth all Sikhs should regard the **Granth Sahib** as guru.

His words, as recorded in a *Bhatt Vahi* (a

October day in 1708. From then, the scripture has been known as *Sri Guru Granth Sahib*. Successive gurus had said that whatever they composed, their *bani* emanated from divine inspiration. None claimed any attribute of divinity for himself. The tenth guru had categorically said that he was only God's servitor and that anyone referring to him as *Parmeshwar* (Supreme Lord) would be consigned to hell. In fact, while recensing the *Adi Granth* at Talwandi Sabo, he declined, despite the urging of many

Sikhs, to include any of his own compositions. (These were collated some years later by Bhai Mani Singh and compiled in what is known as the *Dasam Granth*.)

History provides continuing evidence of this credo. In the troubled and difficult times which the Sikhs faced during the declining years of Moghul rule, when they were ruthlessly persecuted and sought to be exterminated, their most cherished and protected possession was the sacred *Granth*. When Maharaja Ranjit Singh (1780-1839) established a Sikh kingdom, he did

The sanctity of and reverence for the *Sri Guru Granth Sahib* is inculcated in the mind of every Sikh since childhood. At every religious function, it is incumbent after *ardas* to take *hukum* (order or command) from the Holy Book. This entails opening it at random and reading the first *shabad* on the page, whose commencement may at times be on the previous page. Except when it is being read, it is always kept covered. At night, the book is closed, wrapped in one or two layers of cloth and again covered. At all times, it rests on a small bed,

Women devotees ask for blessings by touching the forehead to the ground or by addressing the Supreme Being with folded hands.

so in the name of the Khalsa. His daily routine began with obeisance to and reading from the Book. On festival days, he travelled to the Harimandir in Amritsar for the purpose. After British annexation of the Panjab, Sikh dedication to and belief in the living guru continued. The Gurdwara Reform Movement and other manifestations bear ample testimony to this faith. This tradition continues in independent India. So also wherever in the world Sikhs have made a home.

invariably under a canopy, on a raised platform or plinth. In homes which maintain the *Granth Sahib*, the same procedures are observed. In the more prominent or larger *gurdwaras* the plinth may be embellished with carved marble and have an ornate canopy.

Facing page: *On the steps inside the main entrance devotees gaze upon the Harimandir, in reverence and adoration.*

Profile of the
Sri Guru Granth Sahib

The thirty-six great souls whose lofty ideals and exalted thoughts, expressed in sublime verse, are contained in the Sacred Volume are:

Gurus

Nanak	First Guru	947 *shabads* in 19 *raagas*
Angad	Second Guru	63 *shlokas*
Amar Das	Third Guru	869 *shabads* in 17 *raagas*
Ram Das	Fourth Guru	638 *shabads* in 30 *raagas*
Arjan	Fifth Guru	2,312 *shabads* and *shlokas* in 29 *raagas*
Teg Bahadur	Ninth Guru	59 *shabads* in 14 *raagas* and 56 *shlokas*
Gobind Singh	Tenth Guru	1 *shloka*

Bhaktas and others:

Sadhna	a butcher	1 *shabad*
Surdas	a *brahmin*	2 *shabads*
Sein	a barber	1 *shabad*
Kabir	a weaver	534 *shabads* and *shlokas*
Jaidev	a *brahmin* (author of Geeta Govind)	2 *shabads*
Trilochan	a *vaisha*	5 *shabads*
Dhanna	a *jat*	4 *shabads*
Namdev	calico printer	62 *shabads*
Parmanand	indeterminate origin	1 *shabad*
Pipa	a Rajput noble	1 *shabad*
Sheikh Farid	a *sufi*	123 *shabads* and *shlokas*
Beni	indeterminate origin	3 *shabads*
Bhikhan	a *brahmin*	2 *shabads*
Mardana	rebeck player and the first guru's longtime companion	3 *shlokas*
Ravidas	a *chamar* (leather worker)	40 *shabads*
Ramanand	a *brahmin*	1 *shabad*
Satta and Balwand	bards	8 *vars*
Sunder	third guru's great grandson	6 verses—collectively known as *sud* (beckoning)
Miscellaneous *bhatts*	mostly *brahmins*	123 *swayas*

All gurus haved used the *nom de plume* Nanak for their compositions. At the commencement of a *shabad* or *bani*, the authorship is indicated by the word 'Mehla' (abode) followed by a numeral corresponding to the guru's order in succession. Thus, Mehla 1 would identify the author as Guru Nanak. The compositions of others are identified by individual names. The Holy Book was initially compiled by the fifth guru in 1603-04 and recensed by the tenth guru in 1706. The *Raagmala* at the end is a later addition. The Volume installed in all *gurdwaras* and in homes is identical and has 1,430 pages. The script is Gurmukhi, irrespective of the language of the verse—whether Panjabi, Hindi or any other. Except for the initial thirteen and the concluding seventy-eight pages, the remaining compositions are categorised according to the *raag* in which they should be sung. Singing the *shabads* is *kirtan*. Reciting or reading them is *paath*. Thirty-one *raagas* are included in the Book, though the total number of *raagas* according to ancient texts is eighty-four. Six basic *raagas*, thirty major and forty-eight lesser variations or off-shoots—colourfully described as six males, each having five spouses and eight progeny.

The thirty-one *raagas* which appear in the *Granth Sahib* are: Sri, Majh, Gauri, Asa, Gujri, Devgandhari, Bihagra, Vadhans, Sorath, Dhanasri, Jaitsri, Todi, Bairari, Tilang, Suhi, Bilawal, Gaund, Ramkali, Nat Narain, Mali Gauda, Maru, Tukhari, Kedara, Bhairav, Basant, Sarang, Malar, Kanada, Kalyan, Prahbati and Jaijaiwanti.

Ardas

Ardas is derived from the Persian *arz* meaning supplication and *dast* meaning hands. In other words, a supplication to a higher power, not supported by a written petition. In Sikh practice, it is a solemn part of daily life and also an essential part at all ceremonies, of any type.

Sikhs are enjoined to offer *ardas* twice a day after morning and evening prayers. It is also said at numerous occasions as, for example, at the commencement of a journey, before appearing for an examination, on the first day of a child beginning school, or when embarking on a new venture.

The *ardas* is addressed to the Supreme Being, all those present standing with folded hands. At formal occasions, the gathering faces the *Granth Sahib*, otherwise, in a similar respectful stance facing any direction—God is Omnipresent. The *ardas* consists essentially of four parts. The first is an invocation; the earlier part of which opens with the initial portion of Guru Gobind Singh's *Chandi di Var*. This has been supplemented later by inclusion of his own name and that of the *Granth Sahib*, the living Guru, seeking their blessings.

The second segment is historical in perspective and recalls the heroic sacrifices made by those true to the faith in the cause of righteousness and defense of the *dharma*; the Five Beloved *(Panj Piarey)* the four sons of the tenth guru, the forty martyrs and numerous others who resisted tyranny and injustice, suffering terrible torture and death at the hands of oppressors, without renouncing their faith. Additions from time to time ensure a historical continuum and recognition of a brotherhood transcending time.

The third portion invokes the blessings of God on the Khalsa, on all human beings and particularly asks for benign guidance in daily living; protection against the five evils of lust, anger, covetousness, attachment and pride; the eternal glory of sacred *gurdwaras* and the opportunity to visit them. It seeks the gifts of service, faith, discernment, patience and, above all, of the Name *(Naam)*.

The final portion may be added appropriate to the occasion; by including mention of the specific purpose for which the *ardas* is being offered, such as the birth of a child, the marriage of a couple, or other observance or on the occasion of death. At formal occasions the offer of *kadah prasad* is included, asking for it to be sanctified for distribution among the congregation.

The concluding words ask for the eternal glory of the One True Being and seek His Blessings for the well-being of every one in the world.

The *ardas* concluded, the congregation kneels and bows in obeisance to the *Granth Sahib*. This done, they stand up and say in unison: *'Sri Waheguru ji ka Khalsa, Sri Waheguru ji ki Fateh'* (The Khalsa is of the Wond'rous Lord, Victory also is His).

Finally, the person who has recited the *ardas* says: *'Jo bole so nihal'* (Whoever utters [this] will be fulfilled) and all respond *'Sat Sri Akal'* (True is the Timeless).

THE PHILOSOPHY
*

Basics

There are many religions in the world, each based on the teachings of great thinkers or founded by inspired souls. Each delineates a way of living and a goal towards which to strive after the end of this life. Also, the manner in which to meet and overcome the problems and temptations encountered during human existence. These ways are *dharma*. Since religion is a route or a way (*path* in Sanskrit), it has come to be known in Panjabi as *panth*. Thus, the Sikh *panth*: one of the several ways or religions.

Some consider that the Sikh faith is a part of the Bhakti movement. This is not entirely so. Although there are similarities, there are also distinct differences between the two. *Bhakti marg* (the way of devotion) is one of the three paths (the others being *karma marg* and *ngyana marg*, respectively the path of action and path of knowledge) expounded in the *Bhagavad Gita* for attaining liberation from the cycle of birth and rebirth. Bhakti took strong roots in South India in the first millennium A.D. It spread to other parts of the country during the first half of the second millennium.

The Sikh *panth* originated with Guru Nanak. It was propagated and evolved by his nine successors. Their teachings are contained in the *Adi Granth*. The basic beliefs summarised below, clearly point to the distinct differences that define the Sikh *panth* from the more

Facing page: Gurdwara Dukh Bhanjan in the parikrama *of Harimandir. Pilgrims paying homage to the* Granth Sahib *(lying open in the foreground).*

amorphous devotions of the Bhakti movement.

The primary objective as taught by this faith is not to look for a heaven or paradise in the hereafter but to aim for ultimate union with the Eternal Lord, described in the *Mool Mantra*, and thus to achieve liberation from the cycle of birth and rebirth. In this endeavour one needs guidance which is provided by the ten gurus, the epitome of which is contained in the *Adi Granth*, the Eternal Guru. Explanation and interpretation of the Sikh *panth* is given in discourses of learned persons. It is beneficial to attend such gatherings in the company of other seekers or *sadh sangat*. The faith is strictly monotheistic.

In the effort to realise the Eternal Lord, an individual has to inculcate purity—of body, mind and soul, both in personal conduct and in relation to society. Hence the advice: *Naam japo* (meditate and pray), *kirt karo* (earn by honest labour) and *vand chhako* (share your earnings). The individual has to live in and as part of this world while resisting temptation. All humans are fellow seekers of salvation.

Emphasis is laid on *udham* (positive action or effort) in any situation. The results are not in one's control. They are dependent on what is ordained which, in turn, is subject to *karmic* forces. Therefore, what is required is acceptance of and surrender to the Divine Will (*Raza* or *Bhana*). Guru Nanak writes in his *Japu*: '. . . countless suffer pain, hunger and adversity; even these, Lord, are Thy Gifts.' He continues: 'Release from the shackles (of the cycle of rebirth) is at the Divine Will; none can say aught else.'

God is not vengeful but benign. Though Omnipotent, He is loving and magnanimous. *Gurbani* names God in some of His infinite qualities and forms: *Daata* (giver), *Pritam* (lover), *Khasam* (husband), *Sahib* (master), *Pita* (father), *Mata* (mother), *Bhandap* (friend), *Bhrata* (brother), *Raakha* (protector), *Meet* (friend), *Yar* (pal), *Karta* (doer), *Thakur* (ruler). In addition, names used by Hindus and Muslims are included: Ram, Rahim, Gobind, Allah, Hari, Rab, Gopal and others. Finally, as *Sargun* (having all qualities) and *Nirgun*

In the endeavour to tread an upright path in an active life, a Sikh is enjoined to be wary of and consciously resist the five elementary temptations or weaknesses of *kaam* (lust), *krodh* (temper), *lobh* (avarice), *moh* (attachment) and *ahankar* (pride).

The essence of the Sikh *panth* then is harmony, universal love, honest labour, moderation in living and complete faith in the One God—the God of all creation; a way which is simple to describe but not easy to follow.

The Granth Sahib *being taken ceremonially from its overnight resting place in the Akal Bunga to a palanquin on its way to the Harimandir.*

(without any attributes). In short, a universal, caring and just God. The gurus refer to themselves variously as *neech* (lowly), *garib* (poor), *das* (servitor), *nimana* (worthless), *banda* (bondsman), *binwant* (supplicant) and in other such humble terms.

The basics thus indicate the need for a balance between an active and contemplative life—one of a *grahasti* (householder) and seeker of salvation (*moksh*), as an integral member of society and being a good individual.

Moral Code

Precepts governing the code of conduct for Sikhs are collectively known as *rehat-maryada* (*rehat*, observance; *maryada*, custom). The essential tenets are derived from the contents of *Gurbani* included in the *Adi Granth*. Injunctions contained in the *Dasam Granth*, particularly those in the *bani* composed by Guru Gobind Singh, have equal authority.

Bhai Gurdas, an eminent scholar and

propounder of the Sikh faith, composed forty *vars* (epic poems) and five hundred and fifty-six *chhands* and *kabits* (both verse forms), which elaborated on the principles of the Sikh faith. He was the scribe who penned the *Adi Granth* at Guru Arjan's dictation. Bhai Nandlal, a devout Sikh and renowned poet, spent eight years at Anandpur with Guru Gobind Singh. He wrote several books in praise of the gurus and on the Sikh way of life. The writings of these two savants rank after *Gurbani* as indicators of the moral code for Sikh belief and practice.

The Shiromani Gurdwara Prabhandhak Committee (SGPC) came into being in 1920 for the basic purpose of managing all *gurdwaras* in India. (This committee in turn constituted the Shiromani Akali Dal to serve as a central body to co-ordinate the activities of various *jathas*.) Not too long after, the SGPC initiated a project to formulate a unified guide for Sikhs. After extensive consideration and debate, the proposals were finalised in 1945 and published under the title: *Sikh Rehat-Maryada*. This is now accepted as the authentic code of personal conduct for

While singing shabads, *the palanquin in which rests the* Granth Sahib *is carried to the Harimandir on the shoulders of devotees. Men vie for the privilege of lending a shoulder.*

Subsequently, several anthologies of and commentaries on Sikh *rehat-maryada* were written during the eighteenth and nineteenth centuries. Some of them exceeded the canons and hence were not acceptable to the orthodox. The more authentic include *Sarabloh Prakash, Tankhanama*, the *Rehatnamas* (of Chopa Singh, Prehlad Singh, Desa Singh and Daya Singh), *Prem Sumarag* and *Mehima Prakash*. Yet all of them remain of secondary authority.

Sikhs. Personal living covers three aspects: prayer, religious observance and *seva* (service).

Prayer: A Sikh is enjoined to recite five *banis* daily: three—the *Japu, Jaap* and the ten *Swaiyas*—in the morning, *Sodar Rehras* at sunset and *Sohila* at bedtime. The morning and evening prayers are to be followed by *ardas*. In addition, a Sikh should, whenever possible, recite or hear *Gurbani* preferably in congregation (*paath* or *kirtan*) and attend *katha* (religious discourse).

Religious observance: To believe in and worship only the One God; to have faith in the teachings of the ten gurus as embodied in the *Sri Guru Granth Sahib*; not to believe in or practice idolatry, caste divisions, untouchability or superstition of any type; to abjure fasting as a religious observance; to abstain from gambling, drugs, tobacco and intoxicants; to keep unshorn hair and not to wilfully harm anyone.

Seva **or service:** To undertake voluntary social service is an essential part of the Sikh faith. This can be rendered in several ways, such as to clean *gurdwara* premises; cook or serve food and wash utensils in the *langar*; to clean the footwear of persons who gather at *gurdwaras*; and to participate in the construction of or repairs at religious or social premises.

In relation to the religious group or community, a Sikh must be an active and integral part of society and the faith. In this endeavour, he or she is expected to contribute both individually and as part of a group towards the benefit of society; and to participate in or contribute towards the construction and maintenance of *gurdwaras*, schools, hospitals, dispensaries, orphanages and the like.

A Sikh is expected to join the fraternity of the Khalsa by undergoing initiation and imbibing *amrit*. The obligations are strict and onerous. Therefore, this initiation should be accepted only after careful and serious consideration.

The rite *(Amrit Sanskar)* is described elsewhere. The obligations prescribed, in addition to those detailed above, are:

(a) The *amritdhari* is henceforth the child of Guru Gobind Singh. Thus, all *amritdharis* are siblings.

(b) At all times to wear the five K's: *kesh* (unshorn hair and beard), *kirpan* (a sword or its replica in miniature), *kangha* (a small comb), *kaach* (knee-length drawers) and *kada* (iron bangle).

(c) Not to consume the flesh of an animal killed in the manner of *halal* (kosher).

(d) To abjure carnal relations with anyone other than one's spouse.

Facing page: As they step into the sacred precincts, devotees make obeisance to the Harimandir.

(e) To eschew the use of tobacco, drugs and intoxicants in any form.

Social and Religious Structure

In elementary terms, a Sikh is one who believes in one God alone and has faith in and follows the teachings of the ten gurus as embodied in the *Sri Guru Granth Sahib*. Anyone can thus be termed a Sikh if he or she follows the basic precepts of the faith. One who believes in and follows the essentials of the faith is termed a *sehajdhari*. Large numbers of people in Panjab and Sindh, especially before India was partitioned, were *sehajdhari* Sikhs. Many continue to be so.

One who, in addition to observing the basic beliefs and practices, wears uncut hair and beard is a *keshadhari*.

An *amritdhari* is one who has partaken of *amrit* and strictly observes the *rehat-maryada* and other injunctions in his daily life and conduct.

Needless to say, there are renegades and apostates amongst Sikhs as there are in any religious or social group.

There is no ordained priesthood. Indeed there is no religious hierarchy. Any Sikh, man or woman, knowing the procedures and able to read the *Granth Sahib* may conduct a religious ceremony.

The authority to pronounce decisions in religious or social matters, to the extent it may be needed, rests with the *Panj Piarey* (the Five Beloved) with ratification by the *sangat*.

Socially, adherents of the faith are meant to be a fraternity. No divisions are recognised on the basis of caste. (Unfortunately, lapses in this respect continue.) Apostates and descendants or followers of those who challenged or opposed the gurus—such as Minas (followers of Guru Arjan's eldest brother, Prithi Chand), Ramraiyas (followers of Guru Har Rai's elder son), and Dhirmalias (followers of Guru Har Gobind's eldest grandson)—are considered beyond the pale for the orthodox. Apart from these, those who dye their beards, those who give an offspring in marriage in exchange for money (giver or taker of dowry), and those who do not observe the vows they have taken or act against the principles of the faith, are *tankhaias* (offenders meriting religious punishment).

Intermarriage amongst Sikhs and Hindus is common, except amongst the most orthodox of both faiths. Sikhs taking spouses of other religious beliefs is less frequent.

The *rehat-maryada* outlines the manner of considering and imposing penalties for religious offences or misdemeanours. The offender voluntarily presents himself before the congregation, acknowledges his lapse and asks for forgiveness. Minor offences can be condoned by consensus. However, for more serious matters, *Panj Piarey* are selected from amongst the congregation to consider and judge the case. In case an offender does not voluntarily come forward, he can be directed to appear before a gathering of his peers.

Penalties are generally in the form of rendering service to the community, such as cleaning utensils at the *langar* or cleaning the shoes of the congregation outside a *gurdwara*. If the case is serious enough, further penalties can be imposed, such as reciting prayers (in addition to the required religious routine), organising a *paath* (reading of *Granth Sahib*) or, at times, a monetary donation to a religious or social institution.

An appeal can be made to the Akal Takht but this is rare. Occasionally, the Akal Takht itself imposes penalties in the case of Sikh political leaders.

A *Gurmata* can only be considered in matters concerning the basic principles of the faith and not in the case of any religious, educational, social or political matter. Such a *Gurmata* can be adopted only by a special convening of a general assembly of the *panth* (*Sarbat Khalsa*).

A *Hukum Nama* is confined to extremely serious cases and can only be issued by the *jathedar* of the Akal Takht in consultation with the *jathedars* of the other four *takhts*. This is done only in very serious matters and is not a general practice.

Rituals and Ceremonies

There are many stages in a person's life—birth, marriage (if concluded) and death—which are common to all humans. In addition, there are other occasions which have a spiritual or denominational significance and are not shared by all. Or, when shared—for example, naming or christening a child—the rituals vary.

For Sikhs, the basic ritual for all occasions is standard. It is always conducted in the presence of *Sri Guru Granth Sahib*. In other words, the Eternal Guru is present and sanctifies the proceedings, whether in a *gurdwara* or at home. The participants at the occasion, whether invited (for celebrations) or voluntary (for unhappy events), enter the sanctum with footwear removed and heads covered. They present themselves before the *Guru Granth*, which rests on a palanquin under a canopy, with a *granthi* (man or woman) in attendance holding a *chavar* (a whisk). They kneel and bow, touching their foreheads to the floor. While paying obeisance it is customary, though not obligatory, to place an offering. The devotees' offering is invariably monetary, the amount determined by the individual. At times, particularly in rural areas, the offering is in kind, for example, grain, fruit or confectionery.

Having rendered obeisance, the person finds space in the room and sits down cross-legged on the floor in a position facing the *Guru Granth*. *Kirtan* (singing of *Gurbani*) is usually in progress. Its duration is normally one hour from the appointed time. At the conclusion of the *kirtan*, it is obligatory to recite six verses (the first five and the final) of the 'Anand Sahib' composed by the third guru. While *kirtan* is being rendered, a salver containing *kadah prasad* (sacramental food), covered by a cloth, is brought in and placed on a stool alongside the *Granth Sahib*. The *kirtan* concluded, the congregation rises and, standing with hands joined in reverence, in unison recites a verse (Ast. 4; v.8) from the *Sukhmani* of the fifth guru:

Tu Thakur Tum peh ardas. . .
You are the Master, to You we address our prayer;
We who exist by Your beneficence.
You are the Father and Mother; we are Your children;
Your bounty bestows upon us countless blessings.

Facing page: *On the causeway to the Harimandir.*

No one can know Your infiniteness for You are
the highest of the high.
The entire universe is in Your command.
Your creation is subject only to Your order.
You alone are cognizant of Your attributes.
Nanak, thy servitor, ever acclaims Your glory.

The *granthi*, standing before the *Granth
Sahib*, then offers *ardas*. At its conclusion, all
in the congregation bow and sit down. The
granthi returns to his/her earlier position
behind the *Granth Sahib*, with reverence folds

equal measure to all present by the *granthi*
and/or voluntary assistants. The recipients
remain seated and receive the *prasad* reverently
in cupped hands. This marks the conclusion of
the service and those attending make obeisance
and withdraw from the sanctum. This, then, is
the basic ritual.

There are occasions when *kirtan* is not
arranged. However, if *prasad* is to be
consecrated, reciting six verses of the 'Anand
Sahib' is *de rigueur* before the *ardas*.

Kadah is made according to a prescribed

Children at a wedding.

back the covering, and proceeds to take *vaak*
or *hukum* (reciting the first *shabad* on a page
opened at random).

The next step is distribution of *kadah
prasad*. The *granthi* uncovers the salver,
touches the contents with the point of a *kirpan*
and places aside five portions, the symbolic
share of the *Panj Piarey*. These are given to
five *amritdhari* Sikhs in the assembly or, at
times, restored to the salver and mixed with the
bulk. Thereafter, the *prasad* is distributed in

recipe. One measure each of wheat flour
(whether refined, wholewheat, semolina or a
mix), sugar and *ghee* (clarified butter) and three
measures of water. While *kadah* or *halwa* is
being made, the person making it recites the *Japu*
during preparation. It is only after the confection
has been consecrated that it becomes *prasad*.

The basic rite can be performed as an
integral observance or as part of a reading of
the entire *Granth Sahib*. The commencement is
Arambh. The conclusion is *Samapati* or *Bhog*.

The rite is generally conducted both at the commencement and conclusion of the *paath*.

Some events are usually observed with the participation of family and friends. For Sikhs, all observances are generally marked by an element of religion. In the case of certain events, there is a prescribed way. For others, the format is left to individual choice.

Birth: On the birth of a child, whether boy or girl, the basic ritual may be organised. Otherwise, *ardas* is offered as thanksgiving and to seek God's benevolence for the child.

Dastarbandi (tying a turban): No ceremony is prescribed for the occasion when a turban is for the first time draped around a boy's head. However, some families organise a function for the event. The extent of ceremony and festivity depends on the individual choice of the boy's family.

Amrit Sanskar (rite of initiation as Khalsa): The ritual dates back to 1699 when on Baisakhi Guru Gobind Singh introduced the procedure to transform five Sikhs (*Panj Piarey*) into Khalsa and invested them with the authority

Dastar bandi: *draping a turban for the first time.*

Naamkaran (naming): It is customary for a child to be given a name before he/she is forty days old. The procedure, preceded by the basic ritual in full or part, involves the *granthi* opening the *Guru Granth* at random and taking *vaak*. The initial letter of the first word of the *shabad* determines the initial letter of the child's name. The actual name is chosen by the parents or in consultation with the family. A boy's name is suffixed by 'Singh' and that of a girl by 'Kaur'.

inter alia to admit others into the fraternity. The procedure continues to be substantially the same and applies to both boys and girls.

The sacrament is normally administered to initiates in a group, amidst an assembly in the presence of *Sri Guru Granth Sahib*. Five eminent Singhs, appropriately garbed and wearing a *kirpan*, place water and some *patasa* (a confection made of sugar only) in a vessel made of pure iron. They sit around it in *virasan* (the hero's posture) and stir the liquid with a *khanda* (a double-edged dagger). While stirring, they recite five *banis*: *Japu*, *Jaap*, ten *Swayas*, *Chaupai* and 'Anand Sahib'. This procedure is normally completed in less than two hours. The initiates bathe and wash their hair before the ceremony. Wearing clean clothes and a *kirpan*, they are in attendance listening to the *bani*, while the *amrit* is being prepared.

When recitation of the five *banis* is completed, *ardas* is offered. Thereafter, *amrit* is administered in a certain manner. The initiates are seated in a row in *virasan*. Each one, in

The initiation rite is followed by counsel on the responsibilities voluntarily accepted by the novitiates. They are also made aware of the restrictions and restraints to which they are now subject. This discourse is followed by *ardas*, to render thanks to the Almighty, and by distribution of *kadah prasad*. The recipients are now admitted to the ranks of the Khalsa.

Marriage: The Sikh marriage is called *Anand Karaj* (pp. 74-79).

Shukrana (thanksgiving): The basic ritual may be organised by anyone to mark an

Kirtan at Gurdwara Bangla Sahib in Delhi: the ornate canopy over the palanquin on which lies the Granth Sahib. The raagis are with their backs to the camera.

turn, receives *amrit* five times in the cupped palm of the right hand. Each time he or she is told to repeat, '*Waheguruji ka Khalsa, Waheguruji ki Fateh*' (The Khalsa is of the Wondrous Lord, Victory also is His) and they respond five times. Then *amrit* is sprinkled five times on the eyes and five times on the head; each time accompanied by the initiate uttering the dictum. The remaining liquid is drunk out of the same bowl in turn by all initiates, signifying that they are now all bound as siblings.

occasion such as a birthday, an anniversary, success in an examination, moving into a new home, inauguration of a business; indeed, whenever moved by a spiritual urge.

Death: In case of death, it is customary to bathe the body, dress and place it on a plank or container and carry it on the shoulders of relatives or friends or in a vehicle to the place of cremation. After *ardas*, the body is consigned to the flames. *Shabads*, expressing *vairag* (detachment), are sung.

70

On return to the house, *Sohila* (the final prayer to be said every night) is recited and *kadah prasad* distributed. On the day of cremation a *sahaj* (simple, easy, in stages) *paath* is begun. The ashes need not be taken to any particular place. They may be immersed in a convenient location which has continuously flowing water or in the ocean.

Lamentation, keening or wailing is not permissible. Death is the inevitable conclusion of birth. It should therefore bring no surprise. As Guru Teg Bahadur wrote:

(i) *Sadharan* (simple) or *khula* (open ended) *paath*, a reading of the Holy Book from beginning to end in convenient intervals. Sikhs are expected to practice this always in their daily lives.

(ii) *Akhand* (uninterrupted) reading of the *Granth Sahib*. This ritual is organised at special occasions of joy, sorrow, difficulty or purely out of devotion. The reading from cover to cover is to be completed in forty-eight hours, in relay by a group which need not comprise any specific number of people. Ideally, the *paath*

In the Harimandir a devotee offers a personal ardas.

Chinta ta ki keejiye jo anhoni hoey
Eh marag sansar ko Nanak thir nahin koey
Be concerned about that which is abnormal.
This (death) is the way of the world,
O Nanak, there are no exceptions.

The conclusion of the *paath* is on the tenth day when the basic ritual is organised. No further observance is required.

Basically there are two methods of conducting a *paath*:

should be undertaken by members of a family or a group from the *sangat*. However, this has now given place to *paathis* who are paid to undertake the *paath*.

Another method followed at times is the *Saptah Paath* which is to be completed in seven days by one or more readers.

Following pages 72-73: *Smearing* haldi *(turmeric) paste on a bridegroom . . . part of the pre-wedding revelry.*

Anand Karaj
The Sikh Marriage Ceremony

Karaj (derived from the Sanskrit *karya*) means literally work or undertaking. In a solemn sense, it also means 'ceremony'. *Anand* is also a Sanskrit word and means literally 'satisfaction' or 'bliss'.

Marriage according to this rite has been sporadically practised amongst Sikhs since the 17th century. In modern times, legal sanction was accorded to it in October 1909 when the Anand Marriage Act was promulgated.

In the case of arranged marriages, the parents of the boy and girl meet to signify mutual consent to the match and to discuss details of the ceremony. No dowry is demanded or given. (Of course, there are glaring exceptions to this custom in present times. Those observing this rule are, however, still to be found.)

A Sikh marriage is not a sacrament or a contract. It is an act of spiritual union, which is accorded religious sanction, and which is consciously and voluntarily embraced by the boy and girl in the solemn presence of the *Granth Sahib.*

The ceremonial for the marriage begins with the arrival of the *barat* (the bridegroom and his parents, accompanied by relatives and friends) at the place of the marriage (the bride's home or a *gurdwara* or any other designated place). The bride's parents, relatives and friends await them at the entrance to the premises. The bridegroom's party stops a few steps away. The following *shabad* is then recited in unison:

Raag Suhi
(Composed by Guru Nanak)
Hum ghar saajan aye

* * * *

Friends have come to our home;
The True One has brought about this meeting.
Through love have we met by the Lord's Grace, and we derive joy by meeting good souls;
Thus have we attained that for which we
    yearned.
The wish is to meet every day, my home is
    blessed;

Within me unending music is sounding, for
    Friends have come to our home.

After the *shabad* has been recited, *ardas* is offered.

Then the *milni*, or meeting, takes place. Essentially, it is between the father of the boy and the father of the girl. But, in some cases, it is extended to include some corresponding male relatives of the couple-to-be, for example, grandfather, uncles and brothers. The fathers (and any others agreed for *milni*) garland each other and embrace. The *barat* is then escorted into the house.

The party proceeds to the place where the marriage is to be solemnised. The *Granth Sahib* is enthroned on a decorated palanquin. *Raagis* are reciting *shabads* while the congregation gathers and, after paying obeisance before the *Granth Sahib*, sits down on the floor facing the Book. The bridegroom sits at the designated place before the *Granth Sahib*. The bride is escorted in by her brothers, sisters and friends to her place to the left of the bridegroom.

At the outset the following *shabad* is recited:

Sloka in Raag Sri
(composition of Guru Nanak)
Kita lodiye kam so har pai akhiye

* * * *

To seek success in any undertaking, request the
    Lord.
By the Grace of His teaching, your objective will
    be fulfilled.
In the company of holy men, imbibe the
    nectar—the treasury of goodness.
Oh Thou dispeller of fear, protect Thy servitor.
(Sayeth) Nanak, by singing His praises one may
    realise the Fathomless Lord.

The actual ceremony begins with an offering of a special *ardas* when only the boy, girl and their respective parents stand up while the rest of the congregation remains seated. Upon completion of the *ardas*, those standing pay obeisance to the *Granth Sahib* and sit down.

The *granthi* then takes *vak* (reciting the first *shabad* on a page opened at random, sometimes beginning on the previous page).

Next, the bride's father proceeds to a position behind the couple and places in the hand of his daughter the edge of the *palla*, or stole, which the bridegroom has around his neck. (The symbolism is equivalent to *kanya dan* or the western custom of 'giving away the bride'.) This action is accompanied by the following *sloka* recited by the *raagis*:

Sloka in Raag Ramkali
(Composition of the 5th Guru Arjan)
Ustat ninda, Nanak, ji mai hab vanjayi chodiya hab kichh tiyagi,
Habay sak kudavay ditthe tau pallai tehnde laagi.

* * * *

I have become immune to praise and criticism, O Nanak, and have renounced all;
Having seen all other worldly attachments to be false,
I take hold of your *palla*.

The next stage is the four *lavan* (the four marriage vows in verse form, see I, II, III and IV below) and the circumambulation of the *Granth Sahib*. Each *lav* is first read by the *granthi*, the *raagis* then recite it to music. As they commence, the couple bow to the *Granth Sahib*, get up and walk slowly (clockwise with the boy leading) around the palanquin. By the time they return to their place the recital has been completed. They pay obeisance to the *Granth Sahib* and sit down. Then the second, third and fourth *lavs* are repeated similarly; first read out by the *granthi* and then recited by the *raagis* as the couple walk around the *Granth Sahib*. During the fourth *lav* it has become a custom to shower flower petals on the bridal couple as they walk around.

I

Raag Suhi
(Composition of the 4th Guru Ram Das)
Har pahldi lav parvirti karam dridaya Bal Ram jio

* * * *

In the First Round, the Lord Wishes you to be firm in the performance of your worldly duties;
Regard the Word of the Creator, as the Vedas indicate the path of duty and the manner to avoid wrong-doing.
Be firm in righteousness, meditate upon the Lord's Name which the Smritis (Vedic scriptures) have eulogised.
Worship the True and Perfect Lord whose Grace will free you of all sins.
The Lord's Name will pervade and true bliss will descend on you.
Says Nanak, with this First Round, the marriage has been initiated.

II

Har doojdi lav Satgur purukh milaya Bal Ram jio

* * * *

In the Second Round your God has deigned to unite you with your partner.
Submitting to the Fearless, you shed the taint of the ego by the Grace of the Lord.
Deference to the Divine and singing His praises reveals to you the presence of the Lord.
Within and without every soul dwells the Lord and all beings are fulfilled.
Says Nanak, with the Second Round there is unsung rejoicing within.

III

Har teejdi lav man chao bhiya bairagiya Bal Ram jio

* * * *

With the Third Round the mind yearns for detachment.
In the company of good souls, one is fortunate to discover the Lord.
The pure Lord is attained and one sings His praises.
The good souls see the Great and attempt to describe the Indescribable;
In every soul resounds the Divine song, and one recites the Name if blest.
Says Nanak, with the Third Round (the seed of) detachment sprouts in the mind.

Following pages 76-77: *At a marriage . . . the couple making obeisance to the* Granth Sahib *(not shown) at the commencement of a* lav.

IV

Har chouthdi lav man sahaj bhiya Har paiya
Bal Ram jio

* * * *

In the Fourth Round the mind is enlightened
and realisation of the Lord is achieved.
By the Lord's Grace the mind attains bliss as the
sweetness of the Lord's presence pervades
body and mind.
The euphoria of this attachment pleases the Lord
and I am ever drawn closer to Him.
The heart's desire has been fulfilled and I am
felicitated by His Grace.

The first verse expresses rejoicing at
attainment of the Lord.

The second exhorts the being to maintain the
union and never to forget the Lord who is the
Fount of all joys and blessings.

The third beseeches the Lord to bestow the
wisdom never to forget Him.

The fourth advises never to forget the true
Lord, the basic support of all.

The fifth explains that the ability to adore
Him is attained only by good fortune.

The final describes how, by reciting this
bani, one may aspire to union with the

The sarbhala . . . *the groom's 'best man'.*

The Master has ordained this marriage and the
bride's heart is filled with joy.
Says Nanak, with this Fourth Round I have
attained the Eternal Lord.

Immediately thereafter six verses of the
'Anand Sahib' are recited.

Raag Ramkali
Anand bhiya meri maye Satguru mai paiya.

* * * *

Lord, to shed pain and sin, and to attain
bliss.

The next *shabad* to be recited is quoted
below and connotes the joy of the bride in
having acquired a life partner. (Here, again, the
shabad is a tribute to God and expresses joy at
having attained the stage of harmony with the
Almighty. It is adopted as part of the ritual of
Anand Karaj.)

78

Raag Sri
(composition of the 4th Guru Ram Das)
Vivah hoa mere Babula
* * * *

O my father, I am married (for) by the Guru's
Grace I have attained the Lord.
The darkness of ignorance has been dispelled
and I forcefully realise the Lord's wishes.
Knowledge of the Guru's wisdom has dawned
on me, darkness banished and I have found
the gift of the Divine Jewel.
The blight of ego has disappeared, my pain
alleviated as I imbibe the Divine knowledge.

Poori asa ji meri mansa
* * * *

O my Lord, all my expectations and desires
are fulfilled.
I am worthless while you, Lord, possess all
the virtues.
O my Lord, you embody all virtues, with
what words can I praise You?
You are oblivious of my doings or faults (but)
forgive me instantly.
I have been blest with the Nine Treasures (of
Your Name) and am in bliss.
Says Nanak, I have found my Lord within

Parting is such sweet sorrow . . . . brothers carrying the bride to the doli. *A doli is a palanquin in which
a bride was traditionally carried to her new home. Now it is invariably a decorated car.*

I have realised the Eternal and the Indestructible,
who is Immortal and Omnipresent.
O my father, I am married (for) by the Guru's
Grace I have attained the Lord.

Then the following *shabad* is recited to
signify that all wishes have been fulfilled by the
Grace of God:

Raag Vadhans
(Composition of the 5th Guru Arjan)

myself and all my sorrows are dispelled.

At the conclusion, *ardas* is again offered.
Upon completion, the congregation pays
obeisance to the *Granth Sahib* and resumes its
position. A *vak* is then taken by the *granthi.*
Thereafter, while *kadah prasad* is distributed to
all, the couple are garlanded and felicitations
and greetings exchanged. During garlanding,
care is taken that one's back is not turned on
the *Granth Sahib.*

THE FOLK
————— * —————

Their Land and Lives

The Panjab (*panj*, five; *ab*, water or river), land of the five rivers, is the cradle of the Sikh faith. It is also at a geographical crossroads. Incursions and invasions into India traversed this land over the centuries—Greeks, Persians, Mongols, Turks, Afghans. The epic war of Mahabharat was fought at Kurukshetra. The Indus valley civilisation, Buddhist influence in Mauryan times, Kanishka, all left an imprint. Thus, ethnically and culturally, the people of the region are the product of many influences.

The terrain is largely a plain, sloping down from the sub-Himalayas in the north towards the Thar Desert in the west. The climate varies between intense heat and cold interspersed with summer and winter rains. These factors have determined the largely farming occupation of the people and the cropping pattern. The advent of canal irrigation from the late nineteenth century onwards augmented water supply and increased cultivable areas, thereby benefiting the Panjabi farmer.

It is against the backdrop of this legacy that the Sikh faith evolved. The great majority of the estimated eighteen million Sikhs are to be found in the Panjab. Among those in other parts, it would be rare to find one not having roots in that state. Wherever they be they are distinguishable by their beards and colourful turbans.

The Sikhs share many characteristics with their fellow Panjabis. Some, however, are uniquely their own. The historical experience has made them survivors and hospitable; also

Facing page: Listening attentively to a discourse at a gurdwara.

generous and with a zest for life. This is expressed in the old saw:

Khada peeta laye da, rehnda Nadir Shahe da
What is consumed has worth, what remains is for Nadir Shah.

Whatever appeals to a Sikh as a cause becomes an article of faith, to be pursued at times to the extreme. There are numerous examples in history. One of the more notable in recent times is the Guru ka Bagh *morcha* (agitation) in 1922 when, in pursuit of *gurdwara* reforms, the Akalis (the political arm of the SGPC) defied the administration and faced police brutality, unflinching in their resolve to remain non-violent. The government finally conceded the Akali demands. Mahatma Gandhi then sent a telegram to Baba Kharak Singh: 'The first decisive battle for independence won. Congratulations.' Soon after, Pandit Madan Mohan Malviya, in a speech when visiting Amritsar, said: 'I cannot resist asking every Hindu home to have at least one male child initiated into the fold of the Khalsa. What I see here before my eyes is nothing short of a miracle in our whole history' (in Gopal Singh, 1979, p. 657).

Sikhs are generally quick to take offence, also to accept an apology. An exception is when their faith or symbols are ridiculed. Otherwise, they have an inherent sense of humour. It is said that the majority of jokes about the Sikhs are authored by Sikhs themselves. They can be brash, full of confidence and at times aggressive but with gentleness, reason and coaxing will agree to a great deal. Peremptory behaviour will invariably get their backs up.

Historically, Panjab has had an agrarian economy. The people have been good farmers. The Sikhs have also made excellent soldiers. In addition, they are renowned artisans, carpenters, metal workers and mechanics, for they are adaptive, innovative and inventive. They have made agricultural implements and farm machinery at a fraction of the cost of factory manufactured items.

Sikhs have also made a mark in sports, the civil services, industry, the professions, the fine arts—indeed in all aspects of national life and martyrs. While both considerations are relevant in relation to the Sikh faith, there is a deeper and more fundamental compulsion: complete faith in and devotion to God which is basic to the creed. Love implies sacrifice if not total surrender. If a Sikh is enjoined to love and willingly submit to the One God, he or she must be prepared also to sacrifice everything, including his/her life, for that love. Long before the Sikhs faced hostility and persecution, Guru Nanak wrote (*Adi Granth, shloka* 20, p.1412):

A group of women in a procession at Baisakhi celebrations in Anandpur.

endeavour. In brief, they are an important segment of the diversity, or variety, in which exists the unity of India.

Their Martyrs and Heroes

Every social group has heroes. This would seem to be a necessary focus for the cohesion if not survival of the fraternity. One that has faced adversity and active hostility during its evolution, would also have its

Jau tau prem khelan ka chau...
If you are eager to indulge in (the game of) love come join me with your head placed on the palm of your hand.
Should you step upon this path,
Offer your head without regarding it as a favour (to anyone).

Thus, Sikh history recounts tales of many a martyr and many a hero. Guru Arjan was the first martyr of the new faith. Seven decades later, Guru Teg Bahadur became the second. Both could have saved their lives by compromising on principles. Neither succumbed to any temptation. The fifth guru was subjected to fiendish torture before his soul left body. The ninth guru, before he was beheaded, was made to witness the killing by torture of two faithful Sikhs: Bhai Mati Das and Bhai Diala. They all endured their treatment as *Bhana* (the Will of God) and met their end with prayer on their lips.

The *Panj Piarey*, that is, the Five Beloved, who

Singh at Anandpur but some days later returned to assist him at Khidraana (now Muktsar) and were all killed, are referred to as the *chali mukte* (the forty emancipated).

All of them have special mention in the *ardas*.

Banda Singh Bahadur, who was charged personally by the tenth guru in 1708 to continue his mission in the Panjab, fought many a battle with the Moghul forces until he was captured and put to death in Delhi in 1716.

There followed turmoil and conflict in the Panjab during the greater part of the eighteenth

A view of the contingent of the Sikh Light Infantry at a ceremonial parade.

are the nucleus of the Khalsa, are also regarded as martyrs in as much as they volunteered to sacrifice their lives at the call of their guru.

The four sons of Guru Gobind Singh are all martyrs. Ajit Singh and Jhujhar Singh, aged eighteen and fourteen respectively, fell in the Battle of Chamkaur. The two younger ones, Zorawar Singh (nine years) and Fateh Singh (six years), were executed upon their refusal to convert to Islam.

The forty who had disowned Guru Gobind

century. It saw the waning of Moghul power due to a variety of reasons—weak rulers in Delhi, Sikh defiance, the several incursions of Nadir Shah and Ahmed Shah Abdali. The Sikhs were ruthlessly persecuted during much of this time but remained true to their faith. Many were martyred: Bhai Tara Singh, Bhai Mani Singh, Bhai Bota Singh, Bhai Taru Singh, Subeg Singh, Shahbaz Singh, to name a few.

The most hallowed shrine of the Sikhs, the Harimandir, was twice desecrated and avenged each time. First, in 1737, Masse Khan (known as Massa Ranghar), a Moghul official, had the sacred pool filled up and had horses tethered in the precincts. In the sanctum he witnessed performances by nautch girls while smoking a *hookah*. This was avenged by Bhai Mehtab Singh and Bhai Sukha Singh who came to Amritsar, entered the shrine in disguise, killed Massa Ranghar and escaped. They were later captured and killed.

In 1757, the Harimandir was demolished by order of Ahmed Shah Abdali. Baba Dip Singh

Their persecution apparently fuelled their defiance and gave currency to a doggerel (quoted in a Persian manuscript called *Ibrat Namah*):

Manu asadi datri asi Manu de So-ay
Jiyon jiyon Manu vadhada gharin gharin asi hoey
Manu is the sickle and we for Manu the weeds.
The more of us he mows the more we proliferate in every home.

Then there were the two *ghallugharas* (massacres or holocausts): the *chhota* (small)

Takht Patna Sahib: the birthplace of the tenth guru, Gobind Singh (1666-1708). The gurdwara was constructed later at the direction of Maharaja Ranjit Singh.

and many companions were martyred while leading a Sikh force to avenge this sacrilege. There were times when a price had been put on Sikhs and they were hounded as animals.

In 1748 Muin-ud-Din or Mir Mannu was appointed governor of Lahore and Multan. 'As soon, therefore, as Mir Mannu was firmly established in his authority he addressed himself to the task of suppressing the Sikhs' (G.C. Narang, 1992, p.127). His objective was, as S.M. Latif terms it, 'to extirpate the nation' (quoted by Narang).

and *vaddha* (large) respectively in 1746 and 1762. An estimated 20,000 Sikhs—men, women and children—were killed during the two episodes.

Heroism and sacrifice continued during British rule, whether for national freedom or in religious matters. The Kuka movement, the

Facing page: *In the parikrama of Harimandir Sahib. The spot where Baba Dip Singh fell while leading a Sikh force to avenge the demolition of the Harimandir in 1757 under orders of Ahmed Shah Abdali.*

Ghadar (Revolution) party, the *morchas* (agitations) for *gurdwara* reforms, the *Komagata Maru* episode, the martyrdom of Bhagat Singh and numerous others who went to the gallows or, worse, were sent to *kala pani* (incarceration for life in the Andamans).

The gallantry of the Indian armed forces, both pre- and post-independence, is justifiably renowned. In this record, Sikh officers and men in all three Services occupy a proud place.

The call of the country or the faith has always received a ready response from Sikhs.

with a mart where goods, even animals, are bought and sold. Entertainment does not lag behind. Various shows and games are organised.

There are numerous events in the calendar. Many carry a local emphasis. Others have a wider observance. There are some, however, that are basic and are celebrated wherever there are Sikhs.

Baisakhi is the only festival fixed by the solar calendar. It occurs on 13 April. (Once every thirty-six years it falls on 14 April.) The others

Flowers for the faithful . . . Garlands of marigolds, which had rested on the Granth Sahib, *being given to the devout during a Gurpurab procession.*

Their Festivals

For Sikhs, observing anniversaries of historical events is celebrative in nature. Most occasions are festive while some, commemorating tragic events, are somewhat sedate. Even these carry a festive aura as they recall heroic sacrifice. Because people congregate, the day is termed *mela*, a meeting. At times, especially in rural areas but often even in cities, they attract tradesmen. A *mela* then becomes associated

are all observed according to the lunar calendar, hence the variation in dates every year.

Baisakhi is the first day of Baisakh, the first month of the Bikrami calendar. Apart from ushering in a new year, it has traditionally been observed as a harvest festival in the Panjab.

For Sikhs, the practice of gathering on this day in order to pay homage to the guru was originated by the third guru, Amar Das, almost 450 years ago. Since 1699, the day has an added significance since it marks the day when

Guru Gobind Singh transformed the Sikhs into a new fraternity. It is thus the birth anniversary of the Khalsa.

The occasion is celebrated with enthusiasm. *Akhand paaths* and *kirtans* are held in almost all *gurdwaras*. *Langar* is served. Particularly at larger centres, initiation (*amrit*) ceremonies are organised to induct youth (or even older persons) into the Khalsa brotherhood. At some locations, especially in rural areas and smaller towns, fairs are held at which traders set up stalls to sell foodstuffs and merchandise. Trading

November). Since time immemorial, Hindus have observed it as a day to honour and worship Lakshmi, the consort of Vishnu and the goddess of wealth and beauty. The practice of illuminating homes with oil lamps was evidently introduced to ward off the malignant spirits of darkness. It also came to be associated with the return to Ayodhya of Lord Rama, at the end of his fourteen-year exile and after having defeated Ravana in an epic battle—a celebration of the victory of good over evil.

Guru Amar Das had initiated the practice of

Distribution of kadah prasad *at the conclusion of a religious ceremony.*

of cattle, animal races, wrestling contests, and other sporting events are organised.

Subsequent events which occurred on this day have added to its notability. Special mention is merited of Jalianvala Bagh in Amritsar where, on this day in 1919, a group of unarmed civilians, for the major part Sikhs, became targets of imperial bullets.

Divali or Dipavali, the festival of lights, is celebrated on Amavasya (the last day of the waning moon) in the month of Kartik (October-

asking Sikhs to come to Goindval on the occasion of Divali in addition to Baisakhi. Thus the day had already become an annual occasion for Sikhs to congregate at the seat of the gurus.

In the early seventeenth century, around 1620, the return to Amritsar of Guru Har Gobind after his release from the Fort at Gwalior, coincided with this day. The revered Sikh, Baba Buddha,

Following pages 88-89: *Bullock-cart race; part of rural sports.*

established the practice of illuminating the town of Amritsar to commemorate the occasion. *Gurdwaras* and Sikh homes are widely illuminated on the night of Divali.

Hola Mohalla is a fete introduced in the year 1700 by Guru Gobind Singh. Since then it has been an important annual feature in the Sikh calendar.

Holi is an old springtime festival, centred on recalling the frolicking of Lord Krishna. It is observed on the full moon day of the month of Chet (March-April). People traditionally indulge

means the place of attack. Thus, *hola mohalla;* that is attack and the place of attack.

The purpose was to instruct and drill his followers in the art of warfare. Competitions were held in wrestling, archery, manual combat with sword and shield, combat on horseback, dagger play, and so on. War games and competitions took place. Teams were constituted led by renowned captains—one to attack a location defended by the other. The guru himself observed the manoeuvers and adjudged. Thus he prepared his followers for

Preparations for the langar.

in sprinking colour, liquid or powder, on each other in gay abandon, accompanied by other manifestations of gaiety and revelry.

The tenth guru considered this to be somewhat frivolous. Consequently, he decided to introduce a more purposeful observance of the advent of spring. It was designated on the day after Holi and held at Holgarh, a fort at Anandpur. He devised an observance centred on manly pursuits. The word *hola* is adapted from *halla*, meaning attack, while *mohalla*

the challenges of armed struggle which he undoubtedly foresaw to be in the offing.

The day has certainly lost its original military significance. Nevertheless, it has retained the flavour of its origin. Large numbers still assemble especially at Anandpur to celebrate this festival. Nihangs (a particular group of Sikhs) in their panoply, reminiscent of their original role, congregate at Anandpur. Colourful processions are seen. Displays of horsemanship, tent-pegging and mock-combat are held.

Competitions in various skills, including *gatka* (a preliminary training for fighting with a mace), are organised. Now a *mela* in essence but with a meaningful historical background, the day is celebrated at other places also though perhaps with lesser display.

Gurpurab is the observance of an event related to the lives of the gurus. Four amongst them have a pre-eminence.

The principal Gurpurab is the birth anniversary of Guru Nanak, the founder of the faith. This is universally celebrated, wherever there are Sikhs,

waxing moon in the month of Maghar (November-December). While it is widely observed, the focus centres on *gurdwaras* Sis Ganj and Rakab Ganj in Delhi.

The birth anniversary of Guru Gobind Singh is celebrated on the seventh day of the waxing moon in the month of Poh (December-January).

Other days observed are the anniversaries of the birth, installation and death of the gurus, as also some historic occasions, such as the installation of the *Granth Sahib* in Harimandir. So also the day on which the tenth guru

Holi revelry. Two friends throwing red powder on each other.

on the full moon day of the month of Kartik (October-November).

The anniversary of Guru Arjan's martyrdom falls on the fourth day of the waxing moon in the month of Jesht (May-June). A distinctive feature of this observance is the setting up of *chhabils* (locations where drinking water is available). Cool water, invariably sweetened, is served by volunteers to wayfarers and passersby.

The anniversary of Guru Teg Bahadur's martyrdom occurs on the fifth day of the

designated the Holy Book as the eternal Guru and the martyrdom days of the tenth guru's four young sons.

Their Diaspora

The Sikh faith originated and grew in the Panjab. It is in this land therefore that Sikhs, wherever they be, have their roots.

For a variety of reasons, not least their sense of boldness, some ventured out from their homes.

The partition of the country in 1947, when Panjab was divided, gave an impetus to migration to other parts of India and to other countries.

The earliest moves abroad commenced in the latter part of the nineteenth century. Sikhs went to Britain, Canada, and California. Some were taken by the British to Hongkong and Shanghai as policemen. East Africa became a destination in the wake of the railway being built there. Some went to Panama when the canal was being constructed. Many moved to Thailand, Malaysia, Singapore and Indonesia as traders in

other parts of the world: Nepal, Japan, Australia, New Zealand and a scattering in some South American countries.

Wherever they are present in sufficient numbers, they have built *gurdwaras*, more than one in many cities. Where there is an inadequate number, the *Granth Sahib* is likely to be kept in individual homes.

As for their occupations, Sikhs have made an acceptable place for themselves wherever they are. In many countries, they are into the second or even third generation. Many have achieved

A group of young American Sikhs on a visit to Anandpur.

textiles. Sikhs also went to Afghanistan, Iran, Iraq, Burma (now Myanmar), the Philippines, China and to many countries in the erstwhile British Empire. Sikhs are now also to be found in several countries in Europe, like France, Germany, Italy, Belgium. They are also found in

Previous pages 92-93: *Tent pegging. Part of the festival of Hola Mohalla at Anandpur.*
Facing page: *A young girl carrying a* sarangi *(a string instrument) being tuned by the teacher.*

outstanding success. There was a Sikh Member of Congress in the United States. Sikhs are Members of Parliament in London and Ottawa, and members of municipal bodies in some countries. They are successful businessmen, lawyers, judges, physicians, surgeons, architects, engineers and other professionals in many countries, also civil servants in some. Many have made a notable contribution to the societies in which they live.